STRATEGIC PLANNING:

The ASTD Trainer's Sourcebook

Books in The ASTD Trainer's Sourcebook Series

STRATEGIC PLANNING:

The ASTD Trainer's Sourcebook

John C. Wills

McGraw-Hill

New York San Francisco Washington D.C. Auckland Bogotá
Caracas Lisbon London Madrid Mexico City Milan
Montreal New Delhi San Juan Singapore
Sydney Tokyo Toronto

Library of Congress Catalog Card Number: 96-77803

ISBN 0-07-053442-X

 This book is printed on recycled, acid-free paper containing a minimum of 50% recycled de-inked fiber.

Sourcebook Team:

Co-Publishers:	Philip Ruppel, Training McGraw-Hill
	Nancy Olson, American Society for Training and Development
Acquisitions Editor:	Richard Narramore, Training McGraw-Hill
Editing Supervisor:	Paul R. Sobel, McGraw-Hill Professional Book Group
Production Supervisor:	Donald F. Schmidt, McGraw-Hill Professional Book Group
Series Advisor:	Richard L. Roe
Editing/Imagesetting:	Bill McLaughlin, Advanced Communications;
	Deborah Stockton, DOS Enterprises;
	Kalista Johnson-Nash

Contents

Preface

I'd like to tell you how this series came about. As a longtime editor and resource person in the training and development field, I was frequently asked by trainers, facilitators, consultants, and instructors to provide them with training designs on a variety of topics. These customers wanted one-hour, half-day, and full-day programs on such topics as team-building, coaching, diversity, supervision, and sales. Along with the training designs, they required facilitator notes, participant handouts, flipchart ideas, games, activities, structured experiences, overhead transparencies, and instruments. But, that wasn't all. They wanted to be able to reproduce, customize, and adapt these materials to their particular needs—at no cost!

Later, as an independent editor, I shared these needs with Nancy Olson, the publisher at the American Society for Training and Development. Nancy mentioned that ASTD received many similar calls from facilitators who were looking for a basic library of reproducible training materials. Many of the classic training volumes, such as Newstrom and Scannell's *Games Trainers Play,* provided a variety of useful activities. However, they lacked training designs, handouts, overheads, and instruments—and, most importantly, they tended to be organized by method rather than by topic. You can guess the rest of the story: Welcome to *The ASTD Trainer's Sourcebook.*

This sourcebook is part of an open-ended series that covers the training topics most often found in many organizations. Instead of locking you into a prescribed "workbook mentality," this sourcebook will free you from having to buy more workbooks each time you present training. This volume contains everything you need—background information on the topic, facilitator notes, training designs, participant handouts, activities, instruments, flipcharts, overheads, and resources—and it's all reproducible! We welcome you to adapt it to your particular needs. Please read the copyright limitations on page iv, then photocopy ... edit ... add your name ... add your client's name. Please don't tell us ... it isn't necessary! Enjoy.

Richard L. Roe
ASTD Sourcebook Series Advisor

Chapter One:

Introduction

Welcome to *Strategic Planning: The ASTD Trainer's Sourcebook*—your source for basic strategic planning materials. You can use these *as is* or customize them to meet specific needs.

This Chapter

...serves these purposes:

Establishes some background information about strategic planning and defines biases that influenced this book.

Provides a description of the contents of the book and how its parts relate.

Sets the stage for what you need to do to get ready to conduct the sessions included in this book.

Strategic Planning—Some Thoughts

A strategic planning session should help participants develop plans of action that will move their organizations toward success. There also are

Project plans

Tactical plans

This book provides an approach to conducting the strategic planning efforts needed to help organizations take a longer term view of the activities needed to achieve positive long-term results for their organization.

A strategic planning session is **not** a training session.

Training delivers information that is important to an audience. Traditionally it helps participants develop skills that enhance performance. Admittedly, improved personal performance can contribute to an organization's future success, but *training* typically focuses on *personal performance*.

Strategic planning focuses on *organizational* success. *The purpose of strategic planning sessions is to elicit from participants a plan which will lead the organization in an effective new strategic direction.* Strategic planning is appropriate to both profit and nonprofit-oriented organizations.

What's in This Book?

This book helps you design and deliver strategic planning sessions lasting:

One-hour
One-half-day
One-day.

Each session focuses on one or more of the following aspects of *strategic planning*:

- Appreciate its *value*

- Realize its *need*

- *Develop* a strategic plan.

These sessions can help an organization define the requirements for future success. In addition to the three sessions identified above, there is also a *"Strategic Planning Activities"* chapter. These activities help you either:

Hone your own skills and understanding of underlying concepts,

Or you can use them with strategic planning groups within your organization.

The Book's Focus

This book focuses on strategic planning. We do not concern ourselves with issues that are necessary to convert the strategic plan into the series of tactical plans and project plans that are required to realize the *vision* created during a strategic planning process. That conversion is an additional effort based on the organization achieving a shared view of this *vision* and a series of tactical plans for achieving it.

Many reasons are typically given for *not* planning. In fact, we could write a book on that topic alone, if one doesn't already exist. Our premise is that planning is necessary to achieve what you set out to accomplish. It is a pro-active approach to defining targeted outcomes. It recognizes the need to be ready to react to situations that are unexpected. But it focuses on reacting within the context of an overall organization target, supported by a set of *strategic, tactical,* and *project* plans.

A story from *Alice in Wonderland* supports this approach. You might remember the part, paraphrased below, where Alice was walking through a forest and suddenly came upon a very large tree at a crossroads.

> From nowhere, a Cheshire cat appeared in the tree and asked Alice, "Can I help you?"
>
> Alice said, "Yes, please. I'm lost and need to know which road I should take."
>
> The Cheshire cat asked, "Where are you going?"
>
> Alice said, "Gee, I don't know!"
>
> "Well," said the Cheshire cat, "then it doesn't matter which road you take."

One important aspect of planning is that it helps you get where you want to go, and to know when you get there. We believe this is far better than just getting where you end up and wondering if that is where you wanted to be, or complaining that you really wish you were somewhere else.

Strategic Planning—Issues

We need to address a couple of issues before you begin using these materials:

"Strategic Planning Is a Journey" on page 3
"Types of Plans" on page 4.

Let's look at these.

Strategic Planning Is a Journey

When you start creating a strategic plan you begin (or continue) a long journey. A strategic planning session accomplishes a number of objectives. These include:

- Improving communication between cross-functional organization management personnel

- Clarifying organizational culture, directions, roles, and responsibilities

- Clarifying terminology used within the organization

- Establishing a common (shared) vision for the organization to pursue—one that meets both the needs of the institution and its groups and individuals.

These sessions can help energize the journey. They also help management identify: *where* to go, and *who can help* achieve the vision.

Types of Plans

Although our focus in this book is on *strategic* plans, at any given time there may be several types of planning occurring within an organization. We examine several types of plans here, so you see how they fit in with and relate to strategic plans.

Each of these plan types has a different approach and purpose. Here is the way the terms are used within this book.

Project plan

The *detailed activities, responsible individuals*, and *timings* required to complete a specific project, such as a task force's three-month human resources assessment.

Project plans are the most commonly developed plans and, therefore, are the type of planning most of us have the most experience doing. Project plans have tangible and measurable outcomes. The duration is generally fixed, with a specified starting date and a targeted completion date. The *project plan* has served us well in completing projects such as the design and development of a training program, or organizing and conducting an organization's annual sales conference.

Tactical and *strategic plans* have the same general objective as the *project plan*, but generally have different planning time frames and, as a result, different levels of specificity.

Tactical plan

The overall activities, measurable outcomes, responsible individuals, and targeted completion dates required to succeed during a relatively short period of time, such as an organization's one-year budgeting cycle or a task force's fifteen-month charter to restructure the organization's human resources.

The organization's *tactical plan* defines the outcomes required for the organization to be successful during the year. To achieve the *tactical plan*'s outcomes it is generally necessary to develop a number of *project plans*. The *tactical plan* must be monitored regularly during the year (monthly or quarterly) to measure progress toward the targeted outcomes, to reassess priorities, to redeploy resources, and to make other necessary adjustments.

Strategic plan

The overall directions and targeted outcomes required to achieve the organization's mission. A *strategic plan* requires the organization to take a longer-term perspective than normally considered necessary for operational situations. It might, for instance, define what business the organization will need to be in to meet competitive pressures in the foreseeable future.

An organization's *strategic plan* defines the outcomes required to successfully achieve its targeted outcomes over a time frame, typically three to five years. To achieve the targeted outcomes it is generally necessary to develop a number of *tactical plans*. The *strategic plan* must be monitored regularly (quarterly or annually) to measure progress, reassess priorities, and make other necessary adjustments.

Needless to say, *project, tactical*, and *strategic* plans should not be static documents. Each needs to be a dynamic description of what the organization is trying to achieve during the specified time frame. Also, all of the organization's plans should reflect and support what the organization is trying to accomplish.

Critical Success Factors

Once an organization has decided to develop a strategic plan to help establish their future directions (or, in some cases, to help them survive in today's uncertain business climate), a number of factors will influence the organization's success or failure. These *critical success factors* (CSFs) include:

"Planning—a Team Effort" on page 5
"The Executive Sponsor" on page 6
"The Stakeholder Group" on page 6
"The Planning Process" on page 7
"Trainer's vs. Facilitator's Role" on page 7
"Training Programs vs. Strategic Planning Sessions" on page 9.

Let's look at each of these.

Planning—a Team Effort

Developing a strategic plan on your own is a quick way to create a document that will have little or no chance of being implemented. The organization's strategic plan must represent the views of your organization's primary stakeholders. Your organization's stakeholders include individuals and representatives from other organizations who will be affected by your organization's successes and failures.

Your challenge is to identify a core planning group that is representative of your organization's primary stakeholders. The core planning group has the responsibility of working together to create your organization's strategic plan, and then helping gain commitment to the plans from the rest of the organization.

One recommended approach is to establish an initial core planning group that creates the organization's *strategic plan*. Members of this core planning group then identify key areas of individual interest within the strategic plan. They solicit help from additional organization stakeholder groups to create special interest subgroups. They also work with their special interest subgroups to refine their area of interest within the strategic plan. The core planning group should reconvene frequently to review collective outputs of the subgroups. Once consensus is achieved, the subgroups can create the specific *tactical* and *project* plans needed to begin implementation.

The Executive Sponsor

Do not attempt to conduct a strategic planning session without an *executive sponsor*. An *executive sponsor* is a key management person within the organization that wants to have the strategic planning session conducted. This individual must have a "healthy dissatisfaction"[1] with the organization's current situation and must be ready to lead the organization to achieve the vision developed during or as a result of the session(s).

The Stakeholder Group

The participants at a strategic planning session must represent a cross-section of the organization's *stakeholders*. These include all the interest groups that will be injured if the organization fails or might be damaged if it fails to change. Stakeholders could include selected representatives from senior and middle management, employees, customers, suppliers, distribution channels, trade/professional organizations, strategic partners/alliances, and others.

The list of *stakeholder group* participants varies significantly from organization to organization. It is influenced by the nature of the organization, its culture, and its profit or nonprofit orientation. For example, in nonprofit organizations competing nonprofit organizations could be included as participants in a strategic planning session. On the other hand, in a profit-oriented organization including a direct competitor would seldom be appropriate or desirable.

---

1   "Healthy dissatisfaction" is a term coined by Tony B. Andrews, a Sydney, Australia–based consultant. He uses the term to emphasize the importance of the attitude that the executive has toward the changes necessary within his or her organization. An *unhealthy attitude* would be that all hope of future success is gone, or the person might be sufficiently satisfied with the current situation to be unwilling to exert the effort to achieve change. In either case, the strategic planning session will waste your time and the time of the stakeholder team. Without the necessary leadership attitude, the outcome of the session(s) will not result in the actions required to achieve the desired changes.

The *executive sponsor* is a good source to help you create an initial list of those who should be included in the group that participates in the strategic planning session(s). Then, discussions with the individuals who are identified in the initial group of participants can often help identify additional candidates. You may want to review these additional candidates with the sponsor, then invite them if appropriate.

The Planning Process

We recommend these phases:

> *Determine* where you are.

> *Decide* where you want to be.

> *Establish* the approach to achieve your target and implement it.

This planning process can be compared to typical life situations. For example, you want to take a vacation. You begin your planning by gathering critical information.

- Know where you are starting. Otherwise, when you call up your travel agent, you might have to say, "Please book a ticket for me, but I'm not exactly sure where I am going to be starting from."

- Decide what you want to do, and possible locations where you can do it. Until you decide that, it is difficult to even dream, much less get others to help you.

- Figure out where you want to go.

- Determine the difficulty of getting from where you are to where you want to go, identify and assign required resources, and solicit necessary assistance.

- Get on with starting and enjoying your vacation.

Trainer's vs. Facilitator's Role

Trainer's instruct. They deliver content and demonstrate acceptable performance. They can be very talented people, performing an important function in delivering training programs for their organization.

The arrow in the diagram that follows describes a trainer's role

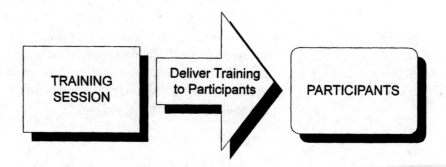

But, the strategic planning facilitator is not a trainer. The following diagram points up the difference in roles:

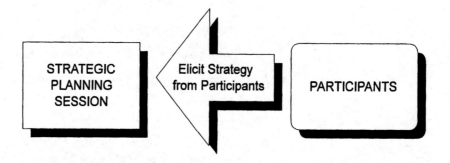

The strategic planning facilitator's role is not a passive one. It is hard work to lead people in new directions, drawing out independent ideas, and achieving a level of consensus. The facilitator accepts the critical role of assisting an organization to make some of the most important decisions they can make—such as:

- What they like about how they are serving their customer's needs today, and want to keep.

- What they want the organization to be.

- How they plan to achieve this future *vision*.

- Who is going to take responsibility for actions that are necessary to start the journey.

When conducting such decision-making sessions the facilitator is *not* and *cannot be* the expert. Neither can the facilitator try to teach. The facilitator's role is to guide and direct the organization's team of stakeholders in a process designed to help them determine what the organization needs to be when it grows up. *These decisions can only be made by the people who will be living (or dying) with the results.* As the session facilitator, you help them clarify their vision and assist them in determining how they want to proceed.

Do not underestimate the importance of maintaining a *facilitation* role. You will find yourself wanting to intercede and wanting to give answers to questions that are posed during the session. That is what instructors do. Your role is to facilitate the development of the strategic plan, to prod the participants when it is necessary to force them to answer honestly. Yet, it is important that the answers be the participants' answers, not yours or the answers that you helped some other organization determine. Your role is to *facilitate* the processes that will cause participants to reach the answers that help them define a future direction that will assist them in achieving future success.

Training Programs vs. Strategic Planning Sessions

Training programs typically focus on the wants and development needs of individual participants. Training programs are delivered in a way that transfers knowledge to and develops skill in the participants. Admittedly, training programs generally benefit the organization as well. They provide employees (performers) with the skills and knowledge they need to help them contribute to the organization's short-and long-term requirements.

Strategic planning sessions are focused on the organization—its future direction and performance, not the performance of the individual participants.

Using the Materials in This Book

The three strategic planning sessions provided in this book are independent units. Each can be used by itself, or in combination with one or both of the others.

One-hour Strategic Planning Meeting

You can use this session to acquaint members of your organization with the concept and value of strategic planning. Use it to build interest in, and demand for, more intensive sessions.

The *One-hour Strategic Planning Meeting* does not provide actual practice in strategic planning. For that, you need to consider one of the other two sessions.

Half-day Strategic Planning Briefing

This session reinforces concepts introduced in the *One-hour Strategic Planning Meeting,* and introduces new ones. It also includes activities that allow participants to practice strategic planning techniques.

One-day Strategic Planning Workshop

This workshop session addresses the same conceptual material as the other two sessions. In addition, it leads to concrete work products: key elements of a *strategic plan* for the organization, and an *action plan* to get the organization moving toward the realization of its plan.

Also materials provide support for each session. They include: *facilitator notes, prepared flipcharts, overhead transparencies,* and *assessments.*

Use the flipcharts and overhead transparencies as is, or tailor them to fit your organization's unique requirements. Each chapter offers detailed suggestions.

Other Support Materials

In addition to the strategic planning sessions, the book also contains three support material chapters:

Getting Things Ready—detailed instructions for organizing and setting up for the sessions.

Strategic Planning Activities—closely related to, but stands independent from, the three strategic planning sessions. The materials in this chapter are designed to allow anyone—reader, facilitator, or participant—to practice certain strategic planning activities on his or her own.

Assessments—these sets of assessment tools:

Preparation Assessments—tools to help you evaluate the organization's readiness for change, select team members, and evaluate a possible preexisting mission statement.

Session Assessments—materials and instructions for assessing the value of each strategic planning session. There also are facilitator instructions and participant session rating sheets.

Results and Progress Assessments—tools to help you monitor the progress of the strategic plan and, when necessary, redirect efforts toward its achievement.

Navigating the Training Plans

The training plans are the heart of the seminar and workshop sessions—the glue that draws and holds everything together. These training plans are set out in detail on a module-by-module basis, with an *agenda, statement of purpose,* and *objectives* for each module. We have attempted to make these training plans as easy to use and as complete as possible. A sample with annotations is shown on page 13. Look for the following elements in each training plan:

1 Each major portion within a module has a section heading and a statement of purpose for the section and suggested timing.

2 Within each section there are one or more major activities, marked by an icon and a descriptive heading.

3 Additionally, you will find a number of supporting activities, each activity marked with an icon and explained with a suggested action.

4 Suggested actions are shown in conjunction with supporting activities, with the appropriate action verb in uppercase ***BOLD ITALICS***.

5 Suggested comments accompany many of the suggested actions. While these comments are fully "scripted," convert them to your own words. Keep the key thoughts, of course, but paraphrase in a way that is meaningful to you and participants.

6 There are also places for your notes to personalize the material to your group and your training style.

Understanding the Icons

Major activities

These icons mark major activities:

Activities that feature facilitator commentary. In these activities, you—as facilitator—present information that will be key to subsequent workshop activities.

Activities carried out in large group discussion. Such activities typically follow major exercises on which participants have worked individually or in groups.

Activities that revolve around table group discussion. This icon is also used as a signal to listen for specific comments.

Activities completed on an individual basis.

Support activities

These icons indicate supporting activities:

Display an overhead transparency. The text accompanying the icon references the transparency title.

Distribute a participant handout, part or all of a learning activity, or an assessment.

Pose a question. Wording for the question follows, as do suggested answers, when appropriate.

Uncover a flipchart, or develop one based on participant feedback.

Transition to another subject or activity.

Call attention to time.

Sample Page

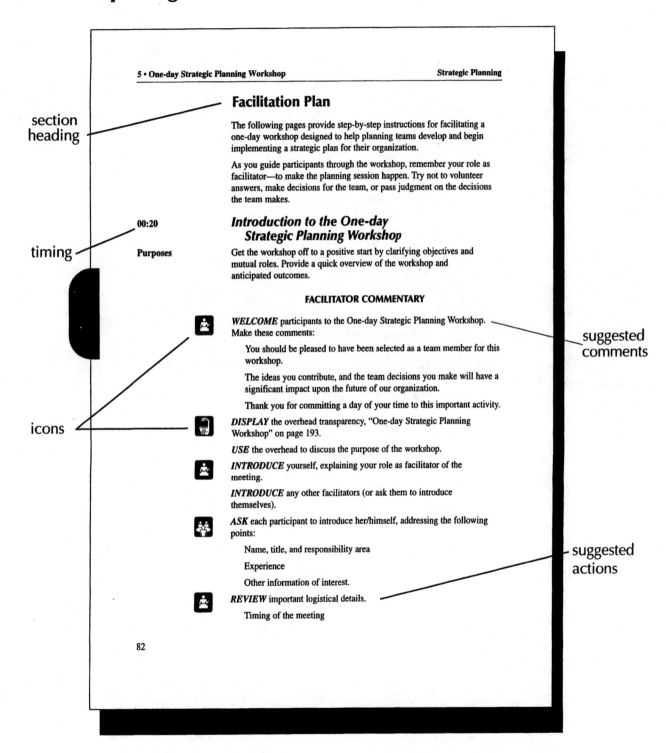

section heading →

timing →

icons →

5 • One-day Strategic Planning Workshop   **Strategic Planning**

Facilitation Plan

The following pages provide step-by-step instructions for facilitating a one-day workshop designed to help planning teams develop and begin implementing a strategic plan for their organization.

As you guide participants through the workshop, remember your role as facilitator—to make the planning session happen. Try not to volunteer answers, make decisions for the team, or pass judgment on the decisions the team makes.

00:20

Introduction to the One-day Strategic Planning Workshop

Purposes

Get the workshop off to a positive start by clarifying objectives and mutual roles. Provide a quick overview of the workshop and anticipated outcomes.

FACILITATOR COMMENTARY

WELCOME participants to the One-day Strategic Planning Workshop. Make these comments:

> You should be pleased to have been selected as a team member for this workshop.

> The ideas you contribute, and the team decisions you make will have a significant impact upon the future of our organization.

> Thank you for committing a day of your time to this important activity.

DISPLAY the overhead transparency, "One-day Strategic Planning Workshop" on page 193.

USE the overhead to discuss the purpose of the workshop.

INTRODUCE yourself, explaining your role as facilitator of the meeting.

INTRODUCE any other facilitators (or ask them to introduce themselves).

ASK each participant to introduce her/himself, addressing the following points:

> Name, title, and responsibility area

> Experience

> Other information of interest.

REVIEW important logistical details.

> Timing of the meeting

82

→ suggested comments

→ suggested actions

Chapter Two

Getting Things Ready

This chapter contains tips and suggestions to help you prepare for your strategic planning session.

This Chapter

... is organized around the following tasks which you need to accomplish in advance of your session(s):

"Meet with Executive Sponsor " on page 21
"Finalize the Agenda " on page 22
"Arrange for Facilities " on page 25
"Follow-up with Attending Participants " on page 30
"Reproduce Facilitator and Participant Materials " on page 31
"Produce Prepared Flipcharts " on page 32
"Obtain Supplies Needed for Session" on page 33
"Organize Catering, Other Support" on page 35.

To help you think through all these tasks, we have provided a series of checklists.

- A *master checklist* which addresses all the tasks listed above. You will find this checklist useful for advance planning and for ongoing monitoring as you get ready.

- *Detail checklists* break out each task. These checklists, beginning on page 21, will be particularly useful if you are able to delegate the tasks. You can provide each an appropriate list.

By thinking through the entire preparation task this way, you will be better prepared to concentrate on the topic, *strategic planning*; you will have less need to be thinking about what you and others have to do next.

As a first step, make one-sided copies of the pages remaining in the chapter and staple them so they don't get mixed up.

Getting Ready: Master Checklists

Use these checklists to monitor the entire process. The "ballot box" column allows you to check off each task as you complete it. The first fill-in column provides a place to enter the name of the person to whom you have delegated the task. The last column provides a place to enter a "must be completed by" date.

Note that some of these tasks will not be necessary if you have permanent seminar or training facilities. We have tried to anticipate situations where you may lack such conveniences and, for example, require a hotel meeting room.

Task	By Whom?	By When?
Meet with the Executive Sponsor	_____	_____
☐ Determine session objectives		
☐ Obtain *executive sponsor*'s view regarding the identification of stakeholders		
☐ Select participants		
☐ Establish date for the session		
☐ Interview key participants to gain background on the organization and environment (if appropriate)		

Task	By Whom?	By When?

Finalize the Agenda

- ❑ Enter session dates and times on agenda
- ❑ Delete events you will exclude
- ❑ Add new events
- ❑ Adjust elapsed times
- ❑ Identify times and duration for breaks/lunch
- ❑ Add start and stop times

Task	By Whom?	By When?

Arrange for Facilities

- ❑ Enter date by which facility arrangements must be completed
- ❑ Enter requirements information
  - Day/date, times
  - Number of people (participants, observers, etc.)
  - Number of breakout rooms (if needed)
  - Any other requirements
- ❑ Verify information about facilities and arrangements

Task	By Whom?	By When?

Follow-up with Attending Participants

❏ Contact those selected to attend the session to verify attendance

❏ Draft an announcement about the session

❏ Distribute the announcement through the *executive sponsor*

❏ Draft a participation acknowledgment

Task	By Whom?	By When?

Reproduce Facilitator and Participant Materials

❏ Enter date by which duplication must be finished

❏ Enter any special duplication requirements (three-ring paper, colored paper stock, etc.)

❏ Delete items you will not require

❏ Add items, not shown, you will require

❏ Estimate the total number of participants and work groups per session

Task	By Whom?	By When?

Produce Prepared Flipcharts

❑ Enter date by which flipcharts are required

❑ Indicate production method

❑ Delete flipcharts you will not use

❑ Add flipcharts you require that are not listed

Task	By Whom?	By When?

Produce Overhead Transparencies

❑ Enter date by which transparencies must be available

❑ Enter any special packaging requirements (mounted, in sleeves, etc.)

❑ Delete transparencies not to be used

❑ Add transparencies needed but not listed

Task	By Whom?	By When?

Obtain Supplies Needed During the Session

❑ Enter number of people attending each
    session

❑ Enter date of session

❑ Delete items not required;
    add others if necessary

❑ Enter when and where items are to be
    delivered

> You probably can't complete this
> until you have identified facilities
> arrangements.

❑ Provide a list of names for place cards
    (if used)

> Allow sufficient time for place card
> preparation

Task	By Whom?	By When?

Organize Catering and Other Support, as Required

❑ Enter date by which catering
    arrangements and other support must
    be confirmed

❑ Enter type of catering desired for each
    session

❑ Enter the nature of other required
    support

Meet with Executive Sponsor

This meeting is crucial to the success of every session. Unless you have strong buy-in from the *executive sponsor*, participants are likely to be only nominally committed, if at all.

In the following worksheets, record the information and commitments you need to obtain during the executive sponsor meeting:

Sponsor Information, Commitment

Needed Information

Information to Obtain	Notes
Executive sponsor's expectations of and objectives for the session	
Name, position, location, and phone number of identified key stakeholders	
Name, position, location, and phone number of participants the *executive sponsor* wants to attend	
Date and location for the session	

Executive Sponsor Commitment

Commitment to Obtain	Notes
Willingness to send session information to participants, or to send "through" his/her office	
Willingness to ensure each participant's attendance at the full session	

Finalize the Agenda

Agendas for each strategic planning session are in this section. These are based on the timings included in the related chapters. Use these pages as a basis for completing your agendas.

Finalize Agenda, One-hour Strategic Planning Meeting

Session Day/Date	Begin Time	Break Time	End Time

	Timing[1]	Start	Stop
"General Orientation" on page 41	00:04		
"Meeting Objectives" on page 42	00:04		
"Types of Plans" on page 42	00:10		
"The Strategic Planning Approach" on page 44	00:08		
"Implement Phase I" on page 45	00:10		
"Implement Phase II" on page 46	00:10		
"Implement Phase III" on page 47	00:10		
"Where to from Here?" on page 49	00:04		

1   Suggested elapsed time

Finalize Agenda, Half-day Strategic Planning Briefing

Session Day/Date	Begin Time	Break Time	End Time

	Timing[1]	Start	Stop
"Introduction, Half-day Strategic Planning Briefing" on page 52	00:15		
"Meeting a Changing World" on page 54	00:30		
"Organizational Growth Cycle" on page 58	00:15		
"Some Planning Concepts" on page 61	00:10		
"Strategic Planning Methodology" on page 62	01:20		
"Session Wrap-up" on page 77	00:10		

1   Suggested elapsed time

Finalize Agenda, One-day Strategic Planning Workshop

Session Day/Date	Begin Time	Break Time	End Time
_____	_____	_____	_____

	Timing[1]	Start	Stop
"Introduction to the One-day Strategic Planning Workshop " on page 82	00:20	_____	_____
"Phase I: Determine Where We Now Are " on page 85	01:25	_____	_____
"Phase II: Decide Where We Would Like to Be " on page 89	03:10	_____	_____
"Phase III: Establish & Implement Target Approach " on page 100	01:45	_____	_____
"Session Wrap-up" on page 107	00:20	_____	_____

1   Suggested elapsed time

Arrange for Facilities

Facility arrangements must be completed by _____ (date).

There are two sub-tasks involved in arranging facilities:

Select and reserve acceptable facilities. See "Room Specifications" on page 29.

Obtain key information about the facilities.

Once facility arrangements have been made, do the following:

- In spaces provided, record details about the facilities.

- Communicate that information to any other facilitators.

- Leave a copy of your specifications with the facility administrator— so he/she will know what you expect.

Meeting Requirements Worksheets

Meeting Requirements for One-hour Strategic Planning Meeting

Session Day/Date	Begin Time	End Time	Number Participants	Number Observers

Other requirements

Facility location

Comments

Meeting Requirements for Half-day Strategic Planning Briefing

Session Day/Date	Begin Time	End Time	Number Participants	Number Observers

Other requirements _____

Facility location _____

Comments _____

Meeting Requirements for One-day Strategic Planning Workshop

Session Day/Date	Begin Time	End Time	Number Participants	Number Observers

Other requirements _____

Facility location _____

Comments _____

Information Required Worksheets

Information Required for One-hour Strategic Planning Meeting

Notes

Person responsible for facility:

   name

   location

   phone number

Emergency procedures

Location of restrooms and
other facilities

Operation of built-in
equipment (screens, etc.)

Location and operation of
climate controls

Location of light switches and
power outlets

Information Required for Half-day Strategic Planning Briefing

Notes

Person responsible for facility:

   name

   location

   phone number

Emergency procedures

Location of restrooms and
other facilities

Operation of built-in
equipment (screens, etc.)

Location and operation of
climate controls

Location of light switches and
power outlets

Information Required for One-day Strategic Planning Workshop

Notes

Person responsible for facility:

    name

    _____

    location

    _____

    phone number

    _____

Emergency procedures

    _____

Location of restrooms and
other facilities

    _____

Operation of built-in
equipment (screens, etc.)

    _____

Location and operation of
climate controls

    _____

Location of light switches and
power outlets

    _____

Room Specifications

These are suggested:

Room Dimensions	Front of Room
One-hour session: up to 10 people—800 ft.^{2} (80m^2) Half-day session: up to 30 people—2400 ft.^{2} (240m^2) One-day session: up to 20 people—1600 ft.^{2} (160m^2) Wall space for posting flipcharts—30 linear feet (10m).	Table for overhead projector Table for facilitator materials and supplies Projection screen Overhead projector (and spare bulb) One whiteboard (with supplies) Four flipchart stands, with supplies (presenter and up to three participant groups) Power outlets and extension cords as required

Participant Seating	Other
Minimum table width—24 inches (60 cm) Minimum table space, per participant—32 inches (80 cm) Arrange tables in a "U-shape" or use round tables. Avoid standard classroom or auditorium arrangements with seats in rows.	Seat any observers at the back of the room Break and lunch facilities nearby Arrange supplies on a table near the facilitator

Follow-up with Attending Participants

Proceed with these steps:

Announce
Monitor
Follow-up

Announce

Distribute announcement by _____ (date).

Task

- ❏ Prepare announcements

- ❏ Duplicate announcements

- ❏ Distribute announcements (through the *executive sponsor*)

Monitor

Contact all participants by _____ (date).

Task

- ❏ Track replies

- ❏ Record participant names in a session roster

- ❏ Acknowledge receipt of written replies

- ❏ Follow-up on late/missing participant replies

Follow-up

Complete your follow-up by _____ (date).

Task

- ❏ Contact participants to confirm attendance, answer questions

- ❏ Alert *executive sponsor* if participants indicate inability to attend

---

Reproduce Facilitator and Participant Materials

Duplicate all materials by _____ (date).

Special requirements _____.

Use the following tables to determine quantities to reproduce:

Quantities for One-hour Strategic Planning Meeting

Component	Unit	Number of Participants	Quantities
Facilitator Guide	1 set per facilitator		_____
Overhead Transparency Sets	1 set per facilitator		_____
Prepared Flipcharts	1 set		_____
Assessment Materials	1 set	x _____ =	_____

Quantities for Half-day Strategic Planning Briefing

Component	Unit	Number of Participants	Quantities
Facilitator Guide	1 set per facilitator		_____
Overhead Transparency Sets	1 set per facilitator		_____
Prepared Flipcharts	1 set		_____
Assessment Materials	1 set	x _____ =	_____

Quantities for One-day Strategic Planning Workshop

Component	Unit	Number of Participants	Quantities
Facilitator Guide	1 set per facilitator		_____
Overhead Transparency Sets	1 set per facilitator		_____
Prepared Flipcharts	1 set		_____
Assessment Materials	1 set	x _____ =	_____

Produce Prepared Flipcharts

Complete prepared flipcharts by _____ (date).

Method for producing them:

❑   Hand printed, using pages referenced below as the source of the text.

❑   Flipchart or poster maker, using pages referenced below as the source of the text.

❑   Other

For suggested flipcharts, see:

"One-hour Strategic Planning Meeting" pages 219 to 220,

"Half-day Strategic Planning Briefing" pages 221 to 230,

"One-day Strategic Planning Workshop" pages 231 to 246.

Obtain Supplies Needed for Session

Number of participants and observers _____

Deliver Supplies to:

	Attention	Address	By Date
One-hour Meeting	_____	_____	_____
Half-day Briefing	_____	_____	_____
One-day Workshop	_____	_____	_____

Participant and Observer Supplies

Item	Quantity per Attendee
❏ Place cards with names imprinted	1
❏ Pencil	1
❏ Binder (1 inch spine, with 20 sheets of writing paper)	1
❏ Copy of this list showing what is packed	1

Room Supplies

Item	Quantity
❏ Whiteboard markers, assorted colors	1 box
❏ Flipchart markers (dark color)	1 box
❏ Overhead transparency markers	1 overhead
❏ Blank overhead transparencies	1 box
❏ Spare flipchart pads	2
❏ Whiteboard cleaning fluid	1 bottle

❑	Paper towels	1 roll
❑	Clear tape	1 roll
	Material to post flipcharts, appropriate to wall surface:	
	❑ masking tape	1 roll
	❑ push-pins	100
❑	Elastic bands	1 box
❑	Three-hole punch	1
❑	Wide, reinforced packing tape	1 roll
❑	This list showing what is packed	1 copy

Organize Catering, Other Support

Date catering and other support arrangements
must be completed _____

Catering

Here are some general catering guidelines:

Coffee and tea on arrival for sessions; other beverages and/or snacks
as appropriate

Coffee, tea, and a light snack at an appropriate mid-morning and/or
mid-afternoon time for half and one-day sessions

Optionally, coffee and tea available on a continuous basis

Here are some general guidelines for lunch:

Allow a maximum of one hour.

Consider a light lunch such as sandwiches and fruit, or a simple buf-
fet. This will help ensure speedy service and reduce afternoon fatigue.

All catering should be provided at a location close to the presentation
room to minimize unproductive time.

Do **not** have catering delivered to the meeting room!

Catering, One-Hour Meeting

Date　　　　　　_____

Time and place　　_____

Beverages

　Coffee　　　❑

　Tea　　　　❑

　Other　　　❑　_____

Food Items　　❑　_____

　　　　　　　❑　_____

　　　　　　　❑　_____

Catering, Half-Day Briefing

Arrival		**Break**	
Date	_____		
Beverages		Beverages	
Coffee	❑	Coffee	❑
Tea	❑	Tea	❑
Other	❑ _____	Other	❑ _____
Food Items	❑ _____	Food Items	❑ _____
	❑ _____		❑ _____
	❑ _____		❑ _____

Catering, One-Day Workshop

Arrival		**Break 1**	
Date	_____		
Time and place	_____	Time and place	_____
Beverages		Beverages	
Coffee	❑	Coffee	❑
Tea	❑	Tea	❑
Other	❑	Other	❑
Food Items	❑ _____	Food Items	❑ _____
	❑ _____		❑ _____
	❑ _____		❑ _____

Catering, One-Day Workshop, *Continued*

Lunch		**Break 2**	
Time and place	_____	Time and place	_____
Beverages		Beverages	
Coffee	❑	Coffee	❑
Tea	❑	Tea	❑
Other	❑	Other	❑
	❑ _____		❑ _____
Food Items	❑ _____	Food Items	❑ _____
	❑ _____		❑ _____

Other Support

Item		Comments
Availability of spare equipment (overhead projector, etc.)	❑	
Availability of nearby duplication service	❑	
_____	❑	
_____	❑	
_____	❑	

High-performance Strategic Planning

_____

participant name

High-performance Strategic Planning

_____

participant name

Chapter Three:

One-hour Strategic Planning Meeting

The agenda and methods shown here have been successfully used with small and large businesses, and with the boards of nonprofit organizations, including ASTD chapters, to accomplish actual strategic planning. The purpose of the meeting, as described in this chapter, is to provide an overview of the strategic planning process and to provide key organization leaders a "flavor" for what is involved.

This Chapter

...contains materials you need to plan for and conduct a one-hour *strategic planning* meeting. You may use the materials essentially as they appear, or adapt them to the needs of your own organization. It is divided into these parts:

Purpose and Objectives of the Meeting

Purpose

This orientation session explains the purpose of strategic planning, its objectives, and worthwhile outcomes and overviews strategic planning methodologies.

Objectives

The participant will be able to:

- State the purpose of the meeting.

- List the requirements for effective strategic planning.

- Describe the general approach and list the three phases of a strategic planning meeting.

- Distinguish between three types of planning: project planning, tactical planning, and strategic planning.

- List considerations relevant to evaluating where an organization currently stands.

- Identify and explain the two steps in determining where the organization wants to be in the future.

- Review an approach for achieving and implementing strategic planning targets.

Meeting Agenda

One-hour Strategic Planning Meeting

	Timing[1]	Start	Stop
"General Orientation" on page 41	00:04		
"Meeting Objectives" on page 42"	00:04		
"Types of Plans" on page 42	00:10		
"The Strategic Planning Approach" on page 44	00:08		
"Implement Phase I" on page 45	00:10		
"Implement Phase II" on page 46	00:10		
"Implement Phase III" on page 47	00:10		
"Where to from Here?" on page 49	00:04		

1   Suggested elapsed time

Facilitation Plan

General Orientation

00:04

Purpose

Orient participants to the objectives and goals of the strategic planning meeting; define key strategic planning terms and concepts; overview the strategic planning process; identify potential benefits of strategic planning.

Note: *The following materials are based on the "as is" approach for conducting a brief strategic planning meeting. If you are adapting the approach to meet your organization's needs, you will need to tailor the following commentary to accommodate your approach.*

FACILITATOR COMMENTARY

WELCOME participants to the one-hour strategic planning meeting.

DESCRIBE the purpose of the meeting and its potential value to the organization.

MAKE points about the *purpose* and *value* of strategic planning that you believe are important to your organization. You may want to tactfully refer to recent concerns that have been raised about the organization's perceived direction or lack of one, long-term goals, and the like.

_____

_____

_____

_____

_____

INTRODUCE yourself, explaining your role as facilitator of the meeting. Then:

INTRODUCE the other participants, or alternatively, ask each participant to introduce her/himself with:

  Name, title, and area of responsibility

Experience, other information of interest.

REVIEW important logistical details.

Timing of the meeting

Procedures to follow in case of emergencies

00:04

Meeting Objectives

DISPLAY the overhead transparency, "What Are the Meeting Objectives?" on page 151.

MAKE the following points:

The purpose of this meeting is to introduce you to the strategic planning process. During the meeting, we will:

- Overview the process

- Learn some of the key terms and processes

- See how strategic planning can help an organization identify and realize meaningful, long-term direction and objectives.

00:10

Types of Plans

DISPLAY the overhead transparency, "Types of Plans" on page 152.

This overhead defines four types of planning—*project, tactical, strategic,* and *action.*

MAKE the following points:

Organizations do many *types* of planning—*formal* and *informal.* They use many names for this planning.

It is worthwhile to understand the forms of planning that occur within any organization.

Let's start with project planning, since that is the most familiar to most of us.

ELABORATE on the term *project plans.*

Good project plans define *who* (or what group) must do *what tasks, by when,* and the *task outcomes.*

They address only a single project and, while typical length varies, in all cases project plans extend only through the life of a specific project.

Project plans may be as formal as Gantt and PERT charts, may be written statements, or a project team's mere tacit commitments.

A project plan's *focus* and *time frames* are narrow.

ELABORATE on the term *tactical plans.*

Tactical plans *support* strategic plans.

Tactical plans are measurable, assign responsibilities, and specify completion dates, much like project plans. Details are omitted, however.

Typical tactical plans have *believable, relatively short* time frames such as one or two years.

ELABORATE on the term *strategic plans*.

Strategic plans are those that define *how* an organization intends to get from where it is now (Phase I) to where it wants to be in the future (Phase II).

Strategic plans are the organization's broad, general *road map* for achieving the future vision and mission.

ELABORATE on the term *action plans*.

In strategic planning, action plans are short-range courses of action that are agreed upon and committed to, in preparation for a subsequent meeting of the team.

For example, a couple of team members might commit to drafting a specific tactical plan and having it ready for review and approval at the next meeting.

 DISPLAY the overhead transparency, "How Do Action Plans Relate to the Mission, & to Other Plans?" on page 153.

 MAKE the following points:

While action plans can relate to the actions at any level of planning, project, tactical, or strategic, our focus here is on *strategic* planning.

Effective action plans, regardless of level, should relate to and support the organization's overall mission.

When reporting to the executive sponsor, a presentation of action plans is an excellent way to communicate the team's progress and results.

 ASK this question:

What do you see as the relationship among strategic, tactical, and project plans?

LOOK FOR the following ideas:

Strategic plans provide long-term direction for tactical plans.

View strategic plans as broad road maps, showing general routes and alternative paths, and tactical plans as detailed, *street and lane road maps*.

If strategic planning is to succeed, tactical plans should support, not conflict with, strategic plans.

Project plans describe *grass roots*, detailed procedures, and tasks, which if successful will lead to the achievement of tactical plans.

TRANSITION to the next section by noting the following:

Throughout the remainder of the meeting, our focus will be on *strategic planning.*

00:08

The Strategic Planning Approach

DISPLAY the overhead transparency, "How Will We Develop Our Organizational Strategic Plan?" on page 154.

This overhead shows how we develop strategic plans. We do this in three phases.

DESCRIBE Phase I.

This occupies 5% to 10% of the planning group's time.

During Phase I, the planning group defines the organization's current status and condition. We address the selection and composition of the planning group later.

USE the travel metaphor to explain the need for Phase I.

If you are planning a trip and call a travel agent for assistance, the first question they ask is, "What will be your departure point?"

Similarly, in strategic planning, a planning group must clearly define the organization's current status before planning where the organization should be in the future.

DESCRIBE Phase II.

This phase occupies 40% to 60% of the planning group's time.

The quality of the decisions made in Phase II ultimately impact the success of the strategic planning effort.

Phase II decisions drive Phase III.

During Phase II, the planning group considers issues such as:

- Technology changes and forecasts
- Competitive forces
- Key areas of opportunity
- Key areas of risk
- The organization's future vision
- The ongoing and future mission of the organization
- Critical success factors in realizing the future vision.

DESCRIBE Phase III.

This phase occupies 40% to 60% of the planning group's time.

During Phase III, the planning group formulates strategies to realize the Phase II vision.

During Phase III the planning group begins the tactical planning that will make the strategic plan happen.

00:10

Implement Phase I

DISPLAY the overhead transparency, "How Will We Evaluate Where We Are Now?" on page 155.

MAKE the following points about *stakeholders:*

The first step in implementing Phase I is to identify all key parties who have a vested interest in the success (or would be harmed by the failure) of the strategic plan. We will refer to these parties as *stakeholders.*

Typical stakeholders are department or section heads who would likely be affected by changes in organizational direction.

People *outside* the organization may also be important stakeholders. Here are some examples:

- An engine supplier to Boeing is likely to be a stakeholder in any strategic plan Boeing might develop to acquire another airline manufacturer which uses different engines.

- An influential executive from a public-spirited business organization might be an important stakeholder, if the strategic plan addressed corporate sponsorships or endorsements.

ASK this question:

In the Boeing example, who else might be a stakeholder from outside Boeing?

LOOK FOR the following suggested stakeholders:

Representative(s) of a potential new acquisition.

MAKE the following points about *strengths*:

Strengths can be tangible or intangible, personal or impersonal.

Examples include *having a:*
- *Benchmark* product
- Unique market niche, with little or no competition
- World-recognized scientist on the R&D staff.

MAKE the following points about *weaknesses:*

Often an organization decides to invest in strategic planning because it recognizes organizational weaknesses.

Or it may foresee future weakening.

Typical weaknesses include:
- Late delivery of products or services
- Quality control problems

- Product or service obsolescence
- Loss of key staff talent.

ASK the group to suggest other examples.

MAKE the following points about *opportunities:*

The planning team will also want to identify existing or potential opportunities for the organization to grow.

Possible opportunities include:

- A competitor is experiencing obsolescence, quality control problems, delay of service deliveries, loss of key staff, etc.
- The government announces grants-in-aid for qualified community service organizations.
- For a multimedia software manufacturer, the availability of a nearby computer graphic arts school.

ASK the group to suggest other examples.

MAKE the following points about *threats*:

Threats are the reverse of opportunities. They are situations that could threaten an organization's viability or future success.

Examples include:

- Increased competition
- The entry into the marketplace of new competitors
- A competitor recently reduced their prices
- Public broadcasting faces congressional matching fund reductions.

ASK the group to suggest other examples.

TRANSITION to the next section by noting the following:

Next we will consider how the team decides on possible future directions for the organization.

00:10   ## *Implement Phase II*

DISPLAY the overhead transparency, "How Will We Determine Where We Want to Be?" on page 156.

MAKE the following comments:

During Phase II, the strategic planning team decides what the organization might want to become.

This process is often referred to as establishing a *new vision* for the organization.

This vision is then documented in the form of a formal, written *mission statement* that all on the planning team agree to.

Neither the vision nor the mission statement indicates how to get there. But they do identify where the organization wants to go and what they want to be in the future.

EXPLAIN what is meant by the vision.

A *vision* as we will use the term in this session is a mental picture of what our organization should look like in the future. It may include a view of how the organization will look and feel, and how it will interact with stakeholders.

 DESCRIBE the mission statement.

A mission statement is a relatively brief, written description of what the company would look like if the vision were realized and the strategic plan were accomplished.

A mission statement describes the future direction of the organization.

It should be consistent with the values, goals, and objectives of the organization's stakeholders.

Here are a couple of examples:

- "Texas Instruments' *Enterprise Solutions Division* specializes in re-engineered application solutions for enterprise materials management, electronic commerce, and advanced manufacturing."

- *"Blue Cross/Blue Shield of Maryland* is a comprehensive managed health-care insurance company that manages the quality of health care, service, and the costs of its offerings to individuals and groups. To serve customers effectively, BC/BS offers a portfolio of products and administrative services, with an emphasis on managed care."

 TRANSITION to the next section by noting that vision and mission statements form the targets for Phase III.

00:10

Implement Phase III

 DISPLAY the overhead transparency, "How Will We Establish an Approach to Achieve, Implement Target?" on page 157.

 COMMENT that during Phase III the planning team identifies and describes in significant detail the following:

Critical assumptions about the organization

The *mission* of the organization

Factors critical to the success of the organization if the vision and mission are to be realized

Measurable and/or *observable outcomes*—the tangible results the organization can hope to realize

Activities that will contribute to and lead to the anticipated outcomes.

DESCRIBE examples of *critical assumptions:*

In any planning activity, the planners must make certain assumptions about factors typically not under the organization's control.

They may document some, others remain unspoken.

Here are some examples:

- Our facility will not be wiped out by a tidal wave.

- The national economy will not enter a major recession.

- No major breakthroughs will occur within the next ten years to make our product line obsolete.

- It will be possible to identify and hire qualified, entry-level Ph.D.s in computer science over the next six years.

DESCRIBE examples of *critical success factors:*

Unlike critical assumptions, critical success factors are (or should be) under the organization's control.

Since they can be managed, it is the organization's own fault if they fail to manage the factors critical to the success of their mission.

Critical success factors are the few, high-priority areas which the organization must manage well to be successful. Note the words *critical* and *few.* In identifying critical success factors, *more* is not *better.*

Obviously, the vision and mission statement will dictate which few will be critical in a given instance.

Here are some examples of critical success factors for a nonprofit organization:

> *Funding*
> *Public relations and image*
> *Trained staff with a service orientation.*

 POST the flipchart "CSFs/Outcomes" on page 220.

 ASK the group to suggest some examples for a profit-making organization.

RECORD acceptable answers on the left side of a prepared, T-chart flipchart.

POST the flipchart for use during the discussion of outcomes.

EXPLAIN what is meant by outcomes.

Outcomes are observable or measurable results of the actions you take.

They are evidence that critical success factors are being achieved.

For a public broadcasting station, a measurable outcome of managing the CSF, adequate funding, might be annual contributions increases (or decreases) over the next three years.

 ASK the group to refer to the T-chart flipchart, and list on the other side some possible outcomes that confirm the CSFs they previously listed are being achieved.

RECORD acceptable answers on the right side of the T-chart flipchart.

 EXPLAIN what is meant by activities.

Once the planning team has identified acceptable, desirable outcomes, it can identify specific activities that could be carried out to measure (or observe) the outcomes.

Following this procedure ensures that the team plans meaningful activities, not "corporate busy work."

How Strategic Planning Helps Organizations

 CONCLUDE the session with these key points:

In the absence of strategic planning, at best things continue as usual.

- More often, the organization begins to drift and lose focus.
- Demand for the organization's products or services may change, and no one notices or seems to care.
- Competitors may bypass the organization without notice until it is too late to react effectively.

The organization that *practices periodic strategic planning* achieves a new sense of direction and goals for which to strive.

- They know the end-point of their journey and have an action plan for getting there.
- They have analyzed the key risk factors, both from within the organization and from outside.
- Thus, they are more likely to achieve their new strategic goals.

Where to from Here?

00:04

 DISPLAY the overhead transparency, "What Is Our Action Plan?" on page 158.

MAKE the following comments:

This meeting has provided a brief overview of what strategic planning is and what is entailed.

This is the point in the meeting when this group needs to formulate their own action plan. Do you want to continue?

If so, you need to select a start-up team to carry out the initial planning.

When they can fill out a chart like the one on this overhead, the initial planning team will be on its way.

 ASK the group if they have questions.

THANK the team for their attention and participation throughout the meeting.

Procedural note: *At this point you may wish to have participants evaluate your strategic planning session.*

"Set Two—Session Assessments" on page 136 provides detailed facilitator instructions and session rating sheets for participants.

Chapter Four:

Half-day
Strategic Planning Briefing

The agenda and methods shown here have been successfully used with small and large businesses, and with the boards of nonprofit organizations, including ASTD chapters.

> **This Chapter**
>
> … contains the instructions and materials needed to conduct a half-day (approximately 3-hour) intensive briefing on strategic planning concepts and techniques. You may use the materials essentially as they appear, or adapt them to the needs of your own organization. The chapter is divided into these parts:
>
> "Briefing Purpose, Objectives " (on page 51)
>
> "Briefing Agenda" (on page 52)
>
> "Facilitation Plan" (on page 52)

Briefing Purpose, Objectives

Purpose

To introduce participants to significant concepts associated with strategic planning, and to demonstrate techniques planners can use in their strategic planning.

Objectives

Participants will be able to:

- Define certain key terms related to strategic planning.

- Recognize significant changes impacting organizations.

- Recognize the typical growth cycle of an organization.

- Recognize discontinuities in a growth cycle, and explain possible causes for such discontinuities.

- Explain how strategic and tactical planning can help organizations anticipate and head off operational discontinuities.

- Describe the three phases of strategic planning and the typical activities and processes that occur during each phase.

Briefing Agenda

Half-day Strategic Planning Briefing, 3 Hours

	Timing[1]	Start	Stop
"Introduction, Half-day Strategic Planning Briefing " (on page 52)	00:15		
"Meeting a Changing World " (on page 54)	00:30		
"Organizational Growth Cycle " (on page 58)	00:15		
"Some Planning Concepts " (on page 61)	00:10		
"Strategic Planning Methodology " (on page 62)	01:20		
"Session Wrap-up" (on page 77)	00:10		

1   Suggested elapsed time

Facilitation Plan

The following pages provide step-by-step instructions for facilitating this three-hour briefing. Remember your role as facilitator—to help participants visualize the strategic planning process and their role in the process.

00:15

Introduction,
Half-day Strategic Planning Briefing

Purpose   Get the briefing off to a positive start by clarifying objectives and roles. Provide a quick overview of the briefing and anticipated outcomes.

FACILITATOR COMMENTARY

WELCOME participants to the three-hour strategic planning briefing. Make the following points during your introduction:

DESCRIBE the purpose of the meeting and its potential value to the organization.

To introduce participants to significant concepts associated with strategic planning, and to demonstrate techniques strategic planners can use in their strategic and tactical planning.

> **Procedural note:** *Make points about the purpose and value of strategic planning that you believe are important to any organization.*
>
> *You may also want to tactfully mention concerns that have been raised in the recent past about the organization's perceived direction or lack of one, its long-term goals, and the like.*
>
> *Ideas are fleeting, jot them down below.*

_____

_____

_____

_____

_____

 INTRODUCE yourself, explaining your role as facilitator.

 ASK each participant to introduce her/himself, addressing the following points:

    Name, title, and responsibility area

    Experience

    Other information of interest.

 REVIEW important logistical details.

    Timing of the meeting

    Procedures to follow in case of an emergency.

 POST the flipchart for half-day "Agenda" (on page 222), at a room location where it can be seen throughout the session.

CHECK OFF the box adjacent to "Introduction" on the flipchart.

COMMENT as follows:

    We have now completed session and people introductions.

    Next, we will move to the topic of "Meeting a Changing World" (on page 54).

> **Procedural note:** *You should find this technique useful throughout the session in visually reminding participants where they are in the session and what is coming up next.*

00:30   *Meeting a Changing World*

FACILITATOR COMMENTARY

 KICK OFF the briefing with the following introductory comments:

Strategic planning is critical to the ongoing success of an organization.

Strategic planning becomes particularly important in our current world of constantly changing expectations and requirements.

- Many observers have commented on American corporations' relative neglect of long-term strategic planning.

- Restricting the organization to short-term planning is shortsighted and risky.

During this briefing, we will look at some key strategic planning concepts, including:

- *Discontinuity* in an organization's life cycle

- *Aligning* the tactical efforts of an organization with its strategic plans

- *Critical success factors*—the few things that are critical to the organization's ongoing success; the things that can be managed by the organization to ensure success.

With these concepts firmly in mind, and with some practice, your team should be well prepared to begin your organization's strategic planning journey.

 DISPLAY the overhead transparency, "Objectives" (on page 160).

FACILITATOR COMMENTARY

 TALK participants through the briefing objectives.

AVOID at this time trying to explain terms possibly new to the group, such as *critical success factor*.

COMMENT about the concept of change.

Change will be a primary topic of focus throughout this briefing.

The purpose of any strategic planning effort is to provide a context for dealing with and managing change within an organization.

Change from outside the organization often forces strategic planning.

Failure to accommodate change from outside the organization can result in obsolescence and business failure.

ASK (rhetorically) how many participants live near blacksmith shops.

ASK (rhetorically) when the organization last hired a keypunch operator.

 DISPLAY the overhead transparency, "Change" (on page 161), which shows the Masaaki Imai quotation.

 ASK participants if they can cite specific examples to illustrate his point.

BE PREPARED to offer your own examples.

_____

_____

_____

_____

_____

 DISPLAY the overhead transparency, "Accelerating Demands" (on page 162).

 COMMENT with the following ideas:

The most significant changes forcing the need for organizations to carry out effective strategic planning are *accelerating demands arising from outside the organization.*

Procedural note: *Here are some examples you might cite. Use these if they are familiar to you.*

Try to add examples from the participants' organization(s) or industry(ies). A space has been provided below for you to note your own examples.

Customer requirements and satisfaction

General Motors developed the Saturn to compete with the Japanese automobile industry.

Cadillac reversed a recent negative image, received the Malcolm Baldridge Award for its efforts, and recovered its previous quality image.

Others:

_____

_____

_____

Increased competition

Historically American Airlines and United dominated the U.S. airline market. No new entrant succeeded in becoming a significant, long-term competitor until Southwest entered the arena.

Others:

_____

_____

_____

Cycle time reduction

Ford approached Mazda to support the development of engines for a new Capri model. Mazda's offer was rejected by Ford. Ford continued its typical five-year development cycle. Meanwhile, Mazda followed its own two-year development cycle with development of the Miata and beat Ford to market by two years.

Boeing cut 777 development time in half by adopting concurrent engineering techniques, joint vendor/customer teams, and performed much of the early flight testing via computer simulation.

Others:

_____

_____

_____

Down-sizing and right-sizing

Boston outsourced the operation of the Boston Public School System to Boston University, reducing costs and improving student performance.

Others:

_____

_____

_____

Environmental considerations

Hazardous waste disposal has become an increasingly important issue in many countries. For example, U.S. oil companies are now required to replace leaking, underground storage containers, and to remove and replace contaminated soil at the site.

Others:

_____

_____

_____

Social and cultural issues

Charges of discrimination and sexual harassment in the workplace are resulting in new regulatory laws and sanctions to ameliorate such problems.

Others:

_____

_____

_____

Globalization

Many companies which formerly marketed their products and services only within their own country are now aggressively seeking opportunities abroad. In many cases, they are experiencing both domestic and international competition, leaving no choice but to globalize their efforts.

Others:

_____

_____

_____

Others:

_____

_____

_____

_____

**Small group
activity**

 ASSIGN participants to two-to-three person teams.

ASK each team to identify one accelerating demand upon the team's organization, and prepare to describe it to the group.

ALLOW 5 minutes for the teams to discuss the demand they have identified and prepare their commentary.

 ASK each team to present its commentary.

ASK any clarifying questions you deem necessary.

ENCOURAGE comments and questions from other team members, but as facilitator, try not to agree, disagree, or otherwise pass judgment.

FACILITATOR COMMENTARY

 TRANSITION to the next section with a comment such as:

> Influences and demands from outside the organization are just one factor necessitating effective strategic planning.
>
> The growth and "aging" of an organization is another.

00:15

Organizational Growth Cycle

 DISPLAY the overhead transparency, "Growth Curve" (on page 163).

FACILITATOR COMMENTARY

 COMMENT as follows:

> Several business specialists have observed and commented on a typical and recurring pattern of organizational growth, among them Richard Foster with McKinsey and Company and George Ainsworth-Land in his book, *New Rules for Growth and Change*.

As organizations age and grow, this growth curve occurs and reoccurs.

The curve presents a conceptual representation of the typical historical experience of most business organizations.

- Note that the vertical axis represents return on effort expended.

- *Return on effort* may be measured in terms of profitability, or other results measures.

- The lateral axis represents time.

DESCRIBE the three segments or phases of the curve.

Phase I represents the organization's start-up history—the entrepreneurial phase.

During Phase I founders typically work long hours and invest significant funds, yet realize little initial return. In fact, they may experience a negative return!

The business is dependent upon its few initial investors—their personalities and charisma.

Eventually, if the business is to be initially successful, things begin to turn around.

In **Phase II**, the managerial phase, the organization experiences increasing success, with increasing returns for effort expended.

Professional managers are hired to structure and systematize the business.

Phase III, a mature organization becomes less efficient. Return for effort expended *slows*, or may *decline*.

CITE actual examples from your own and the group's experience.

An example often cited is IBM's marketing of mainframe computers.

- Somewhat belatedly IBM recognized the flattening of their growth curve, and the increased competition from mid-range and smaller platforms.

- They were clearly in Phase III of the growth curve.

- In the mid-1990s IBM reorganized and adopted a new strategic direction.

- Now, they appear to be on a new growth curve.

 DISPLAY the overhead transparency, "Growth Curve Discontinuity" (on page 164).

Frequently many mature organizations, like IBM, experience mild to severe discontinuities in growth.

There are many symptoms, some appearing from within and some arising from outside the organization.

> Costs rise
>
> Returns decline
>
> New competitors reduce market share
>
> Customers demand shorter delivery times and new services
>
> Social values change, influencing the demand for the organization's goods and services.

An objective of organizations experiencing these symptoms should be to begin strategic planning.

They need to "jump" the organizational curve from one that is flattening out to a new, upward growth pattern.

They need to re-exert the efforts that led to success in Phases I and II by "restarting" the organization.

Group activity

 CONDUCT a full group discussion about threats to or symptoms of slowing growth within the participants' organization.

 USE the prepared flipchart "Deterrents to Growth" (on page 223), to record participant comments.

ASK the group:

> In which phase is our organization?
>
> Are there recognizable trends or other symptoms you have noted that might indicate a coming change of phase?
>
> Are there deterrents to our organization's future growth?

ASSIGN (or ask the group to assign) each deterrent they identify as a weakness from within the organization, or a threat from outside.

RECORD responses on the flipchart.

RETURN to the previous overhead ("Growth Curve Discontinuity" on page 164).

CLOSE OUT this section with comments such as:

> This slowing or downturn in an organization's growth curve is a strong symptom of the need for changing operating strategies.
>
> Complacent organizations ignore the signs and suffer the consequences.
>
> Well managed organizations recognize (or even anticipate) growth discontinuity and commit to effective strategic planning.

00:10   *Some Planning Concepts*

DISPLAY the overhead transparency, "Some Working Definitions" (on page 165).

FACILITATOR COMMENTARY

MAKE the following points:

Organizations do many types of planning, some formal, some informal. And, they use a variety of terms for the types of planning they do.

Lewis Carroll makes an important point about the need for planning in *Alice in Wonderland*. Alice was walking though the woods and suddenly came upon a large tree at a crossroads (paraphrased).

From nowhere, a Cheshire cat appeared in the tree and asked Alice, "Can I help you?"

Alice said, "Yes, please. I'm lost and need to know which road I should take."

The Cheshire cat asked, "Where are you going?"

Alice said, "Gee, I don't know!"

"Well," said the Cheshire cat, "then it doesn't matter which road you take."

For purposes of our discussion we will concentrate on two types of planning, *strategic* and *tactical*.

EXPLAIN the term *strategic planning*.

Strategic plans are those that define how an organization intends to get from where it is now to where it wants to be in the future.

Strategic plans are the organization's broad, general "road map" for achieving their future vision and mission.

Strategic planning typically reflects a relatively long time frame, three to five years (or more).

EXPLAIN the term *tactical planning*.

Tactical plans support strategic plans.

Tactical plans are measurable, assign responsibilities, and specify completion dates.

Typical tactical plans have believable, relatively short time frames such as 6 to 18 months.

EXPLAIN the term *project planning*.

Project plans define *who* (or what group) must do *what* tasks, by *when*, and what the task outcomes must be.

They address only a single project and, while typical length varies, in all cases project plans only extend through the life of a specific project.

Project plans may be as formal as Gantt and PERT charts, may be written statements, or merely a project team's tacit commitments.

Project plans are narrow in focus and time frame.

EXPLAIN the term *action planning.*

Action plans define specific steps an organization or group can carry out to accomplish a plan, whether project related, tactical, or strategic in scope.

Action plans provide time frames for observing and tracking activities and outcomes required to achieve objectives.

They are far more than a task, or a "to-do" list. They involve organizing support and commitment.

01:20

Strategic Planning Methodology

 DISPLAY the overhead transparency, "The Strategic Planning Journey (1)" (on page 166).

 INTRODUCE this section with the following ideas:

In strategic planning, it is useful to have a methodology everyone on the planning team supports.

Strategic planning entails these three phases. During the remainder of the session, we will discuss each in some detail, and review some analytical techniques for accomplishing each phase.

 DISPLAY the overhead transparency, "Where Are You Now?" (on page 167).

 COMMENT as follows:

To determine the organization's current status, it is useful to identify these three variables.

Who has a vested interest in the success of the strategic plan we devolve?

What are our current *strengths, weaknesses, opportunities,* and *threats* to success?

What are our organization's core values?

 DISPLAY the overhead transparency, "Stakeholder Analysis" (on page 168).

DEFINE the term *stakeholder.*

As a first step in answering the question, "Where are we now?" it is useful to identify the parties with a vested interest in the success (or failure) of the organization.

These are referred to as the *stakeholders*.

Typical stakeholders are department or section heads who would likely be affected by significant changes in organizational direction.

Some examples of other potential stakeholders include:

employees, customers/clients, suppliers

 ASK the full group:

Can you think of other possible stakeholders?

Could an organization's *suppliers* be stakeholders?

Could an organization's *competitors* be stakeholders?

USE these and other questions you feel necessary to clarify the concept of stakeholder.

Group activity

 POST the prepared flipchart, "Our Key Stakeholders" (on page 224).

 ASK the group to identify the people or groups that represent their organization's key stakeholders.

> **Procedural note :** *Allow about five minutes for the discussion.*

RECORD suggestions from the group on the flipchart.

SEEK agreement from the group as to the top five, and highlight these stakeholders on the flipchart.

SWOT Analysis

 DISPLAY the overhead transparency, "SWOT Analysis" (on page 169).

 COMMENT as follows:

As a next step in answering the question, "Where are we now?" it is useful to review the organization's current strengths, weaknesses, opportunities, and threats to success.

We refer to this as SWOT analysis (pronounced *swat*).

Strengths are *areas of value* in your organization and among your organization's stakeholders.

One example of an organizational strength is staff who are expert in a particular topic or skill.

Weaknesses are *liabilities* that exist within the organization, and among the organization's stakeholders.

One example of an organizational weakness is the problem of inadequate geographical spread—the lack of coverage in a targeted or key geographic region.

Another example is an organization that lacks competencies in key competitive specialties.

 USE the prepared flipchart "Our Strengths & Weaknesses" (on page 225), to record participant comments in response to the following.

 ASK the group the question:

"What are some other examples of organizational strengths and weaknesses?"

COMMENT as follows:

Don't worry about your own organization for now. Just think about strengths and weaknesses in general.

Opportunities represent favorable or advantageous combinations of circumstances that provide the organization with the chance to explore new directions.

An example of an organizational opportunity is an improving business climate.

Threats represent potential dangers that could prevent or inhibit the future success of an organization. Threats may exist both within the organization and among its stakeholders.

An example of an organizational threat is *staff burnout*.

Another example is a *regulatory change* inhibiting the organization's future opportunities.

 ASK the group to discuss the following question:

"What are some other examples of *organizational opportunities* and *threats*?"

 USE flipchart "Our Opportunities and Threats" (on page 227), to record participant comments.

COMMENT as follows:

Don't worry about your own organization for now. Just think about opportunities and threats in general.

Small group activity

DIVIDE the group into four small groups.

ASSIGN each small group either the category *strengths and weaknesses* or *opportunities and threats*.

ASK each group to try to think of three to five examples in their assigned categories, within their own organization.

 POST the prepared flipcharts "Our Strengths and Weaknesses" (on page 228), and "Our Opportunities and Threats" (on page 227).

ASK each group to record their ideas on the appropriate flipchart.

DIRECT each table group to spend about five minutes formulating examples.

FACILITATOR DEBRIEF

 CALL on each group to present findings.

HELP the groups, if necessary, to distinguish between weaknesses from within, and threats from outside the organization.

FACILITATOR COMMENTARY

 TRANSITION with a comment such as the following:

> Another way to look at the organization is to examine its basic beliefs—it's core values.

 DISPLAY the overhead transparency "Value Analysis" (on page 170).

COMMENT with ideas such as:

> Value analysis is more abstract, and in some ways more difficult to pin down than stakeholders or SWOTs.

> But, a clear concept of an organization's core values can serve as a set of ethical principles.

> The organization's core values define what are and what are not permissible directions the team may take in their own organization's strategic planning strategy.

> Core value examples include:

>> Treat employees the way you would want to be treated.
>> Solve customer problems.

Group activity

 ASK the participants to take a few minutes to think about what they believe are the core values of their organization.

ALLOW two minutes of thought.

POST the prepared flipchart "Our Core Values" (on page 230).

ASK for volunteers to suggest one or more core values.

RECORD ideas with high group consensus on the flipchart.

 DISPLAY the overhead transparency, "The Strategic Planning Journey (2)" (on page 171). (This is a copy of an overhead you used earlier, with Phase II highlighted.)

TRANSITION by calling attention to the second item, "Decide Where You Want To Be," our next discussion point.

 DISPLAY the overhead transparency, "Where Do You Want to Be?" (on page 172).

FACILITATOR COMMENTARY

 COMMENT with the following ideas:

> During this stage of strategic planning, the planning team begins to compare where the organization is now with where it could be. To do this they:
>
> • Create a vision of what the organization might be, and
>
> • Develop a mutually agreeable organizational mission statement.
>
> The visioning process entails establishing a *vision* for the organization.
>
> This vision is then documented in the form of a formal, written, *mission statement* that all on the planning team accept.
>
> Neither *vision* nor *mission* statements indicate how to get there. They identify where the organization wants to go and what they want to be in the future.

 DISPLAY the overhead transparency, "The Vision" (on page 173).

 DESCRIBE the "vision" concept.

> In visioning, individuals within the strategic planning team develop a mental picture of what the organization might and should look like, feel like, and be seen to be in the future.
>
> Team members then share their visions and negotiate to reach a common, *shared* vision.
>
> This shared vision will form the basis for writing a formal strategic plan or mission statement to achieve the shared vision.

Group activity

 EXPLAIN that, to give participants a flavor for the visioning technique, you are going to ask them to participate in a brief visioning exercise.

READ the following visioning instructions to the participants.

PAUSE briefly between each statement, to allow participants to relax and concentrate.

REMIND participants that, since this is a visioning exercise, they are free to make any assumptions they wish.

Put all your materials aside.

Make yourself comfortable in your chair.

Close your eyes if you wish [long pause].

It is now four to six years in the future.

Your organization has just been selected to receive the Twenty-first Century Award, the most prestigious citation given to any national enterprise.

Since you were a key player in the efforts that led to your organization's success, you have been selected to appear before a joint session of your country's legislative body.

You are sitting in the anteroom of the legislative hall, awaiting the beginning of the session in which you will accept your organization's award from the country's highest government official.

You have just learned from a key aide that, in addition to receiving the award for your organization, you will also be asked to briefly describe what occurred in your organization over the past five years that has led to this moment.

> How does the organization now differ from what it was four years ago?
>
> What positive changes have occurred?
>
> How were they achieved?
>
> Did technological developments contribute to these changes?
>
> What other opportunities, if any, did you take advantage of?

You review your notes and begin collecting your thoughts.

ASK the participants to take one or two minutes thinking about what they would say, and then to jot down their ideas. After five minutes:

ASK several volunteers to present ideas.

WRAP UP the exercise with comments such as:

> Did you notice how the visioning technique of looking back from the future allowed you to think about a wider range of possibilities? You were less confined in your thinking.

Visioning is a good technique to help planning teams do the same thing early on in their strategic planning.

FACILITATOR COMMENTARY

 DESCRIBE the mission statement.

A mission statement is a relatively brief, written description of what the company would look like if the team's vision were realized and the strategic plan were accomplished.

 DISPLAY the overhead transparency, "Sample Mission Statements" (on page 174).

Here are a couple of examples:

"Texas Instruments' Enterprise Solutions Division specializes in re-engineered application solutions for enterprise materials management, electronic commerce, and advanced manufacturing."

"Blue Cross/Blue Shield of Maryland is a comprehensive managed health-care insurance company that manages the quality of health care, service, and the costs of its offerings to individuals and groups. To serve customers effectively, BC/BS offers a portfolio of products and administrative services, with an emphasis on managed care."

 DISPLAY the overhead transparency, "The Strategic Planning Journey (3)" on page 175.

TRANSITION by calling attention to the third phase, "Establish a Strategy to Achieve Your Target"

EXPLAIN that this is our next discussion point.

 DISPLAY the overhead transparency, "What Strategy Will You Use?" (on page 176).

FACILITATOR COMMENTARY

 COMMENT with the following ideas:

During this stage of strategic planning, the planning team accomplishes these tasks. They:

Identify a mutually agreeable strategic approach,

Identify strategic opportunities, and

Prioritize the opportunities they have identified.

Now we will look at several techniques planning teams might use to *formulate, analyze,* and *test* the strategic approach(es) for realizing the vision.

DISPLAY the overhead transparency, "Porter Generic Strategy Model" (on page 177).

FACILITATOR COMMENTARY

 EXPLAIN the Porter model.

Michael Porter, of the Harvard Business School, has developed this generic model to help organizations identify their broad, strategic approach.

The Porter approach can be used in both Phase I (the present) and Phase II (where we would like to be).

The idea is to decide in which quadrant you are likely to have the greatest success with each part of your long-term strategic plan.

Looking down the vertical axis, you first decide whether success is more likely to come from a *total market* focus, or from a *special niche*.

DESCRIBE examples you know of, or use these:

Airlines

Some airlines provide a full range of services, seeking to satisfy a broad range of travelers.

Some airlines feature *no frills* service, targeting the traveler niche that is seeking low cost travel.

Hotels

Marriott Hotels offer a variety of types of hotels, motels, and suites to attract a broad range of guests.

Motel 6 targets a specific traveler niche, those looking for budget rooms.

Now, looking across the horizontal axis, you need to decide whether your new strategy is more likely to succeed:

If you can keep costs down and/or realize a smaller profit margin,

or

If you believe that customers will place a greater value on your product or service because it differs from competitors'.

 DESCRIBE an example and ask the group to decide which quadrant it fits.

Industry	Example	Quadrant
Automobile	Rolls Royce wants its autos to be unlike those of the competition.	Niche / Differentiation
	Yugo targets low-budget customers who need transport.	Niche / Cost Leadership
Airlines	Offer a variety of passenger choices: first class, business class, coach, economy.	(All)
Travel Agencies	Offer relaxing travel to a single, resort location.	Niche / Differentiation
	Offer educational tours.	Niche
	Feature tours to archeological digs.	Niche

POINT OUT that the model need not apply to an entire strategic plan.

There may be opportunities within one, a few, or all quadrants.

You may assign one product or service to one quadrant, another to a different quadrant.

You may start with a product or service in the lower right-hand quadrant, then move to the lower left-hand quadrant as new competitors emerge.

 DISPLAY the overhead transparency, "Strategic Alignment" (on page 178).

 COMMENT with the following ideas:

This matrix illustrates another model for defining your approach and identifying strategic opportunities.

The strategic alignment model is useful in allowing you to analyze your organization's key strengths and weaknesses.

The model was jointly developed by

John Henderson of Boston University

Jim Sharpe with IBM Consulting, Australia

Marilyn Parker with IBM Consulting in the U.S.

COMMENT that you will explain this model quadrant-by-quadrant.

DISCUSS the upper left-hand quadrant.

This quadrant asks you to examine factors *external* to your organization that are likely to influence the success of any strategy you choose.

It allows you to focus on how a variety of external factors might affect your underlying business strategy.

External factors might include:

> Your customer base
> Suppliers
> Traditional competitors
> New competitors
> Government regulations
> Products and services competitive to your own.

DISCUSS the lower left-hand quadrant.

This quadrant asks you to examine factors *internal* to your organization.

It allows you to focus on the effects strategic changes might have on the existing organizational structure.

Internal organizational factors might include:

> Your existing organizational structure
>
> Your organization's core competencies and areas of perceived weakness
>
> Available people, facilities, equipment, and other physical assets.

PROVIDE an illustration of the analysis of this quadrant.

Your analysis in this quadrant might reveal that the success of your group's strategy will entail modifying the existing organizational structure.

For example, if you plan to acquire a competitor and retain their core management team, it is likely you will have to execute a corporate reorganization to implement your strategic plan.

DISCUSS the upper right-hand quadrant.

This quadrant encourages you to look at potential technologies that might enable you to implement your strategy within each key organizational discipline: human resources, engineering, information systems, manufacturing, etc.

It asks you to examine the existing and emerging technologies that might positively or negatively impact your strategic approach.

This is influenced by existing and emerging technologies from outside suppliers: new investors, breakthrough ideas, etc.

DISCUSS the lower right-hand quadrant.

This quadrant asks you to examine the products and services that each of these various disciplines deliver.

That allows you to verify that each product or service effectively supports the attainment of the organization's strategy, the organization, and uses the advanced technologies associated with each discipline.

COMMENT with the following ideas:

> Remember, the issue addressed by this model is the *alignment* of:
>
> > Strategy
> >
> > Organization
> >
> > Technology
> >
> > Individual units
>
> All must be aligned to achieve a shared vision while satisfying and meeting both internal and external circumstances.

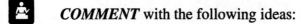 *DISPLAY* the overhead transparency, "Reaching the Vision" (on page 179).

FACILITATOR COMMENTARY

 COMMENT with the following ideas:

> In strategic planning, one of the most difficult tasks is to get people to accept the need for real change.
>
> The top curve is a projection of the ideal results from a strategic vision. It assumes total success, all along the way, in achieving your vision.
>
> In reality, you must anticipate a number of steps along the way to reaching your vision.
>
> As the center curve illustrates, your team will need to create a series of incremental plans, to conduct periodic reviews, and to make occasional adjustments.
>
> Annual plans and reviews with regular adjustments to the organization's strategy are the rule, not the exception.

 DISPLAY the overhead transparency, "Change (Keen quote)" (on page 180).

ALLOW participants time to read this quotation from Peter Keen's book, *Competing in Time.*

 COMMENT with the following ideas:

> The bottom curve on the previous overhead illustrates what is likely to happen if an organization does nothing.
>
> This quotation emphasizes how hard it can be to bring change about, particularly within an old, established, successful organization.

DISPLAY the overhead transparency, "How Will You Implement Your Plans?" (on page 181).

 TRANSITION with the following comment:

We will next look at three techniques for implementing the changes required to realize the team's strategic plans.

Identifying *critical assumptions*

Identifying *critical success factors*

Creating *action plans* to make the strategic plan happen.

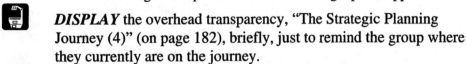

DISPLAY the overhead transparency, "The Strategic Planning Journey (4)" (on page 182), briefly, just to remind the group where they currently are on the journey.

DISPLAY the overhead transparency, "Critical Assumptions" (on page 183).

EXPLAIN critical assumptions:

The few, key assumptions on which your organization is basing its strategic plans.

Some critical assumptions can be verified by further research; others cannot, since they are (or may be) affected by future events not under your organization's control.

REVIEW the examples on the overhead.

Small group activity

DIVIDE the group into two discussion sub-groups. Identify one group as Group 1, the other as Group 2.

DISPLAY the overhead transparency, "Identifying Critical Assumptions" (on page 184).

ASK Group 1 to discuss the first situation.

ASK Group 2 to discuss the second situation.

REVIEW the instructions for the learning activity.

ALLOW five minutes to complete the activity.

USE a blank flipchart to record participant comments.

Situation 1: *Part of your strategic plan will apply an emerging technology. Your organization does not own the patents, but you have a history of success working with the organization that does.*

Situation 2: *To achieve your strategic plan, you plan to hire 120 recent genetic engineering Ph.D. graduates over the next five years.*

ASK participants to select a spokesperson to record their assumptions on a blank flipchart.

ASK the spokesperson from Group 1 to identify the critical assumptions they identified for Situation 1.

LOOK for *critical assumptions* such as these:

> The emerging technology will not encounter any unanticipated problems.

> Your relationship with the patent-holding organization will not deteriorate before you are ready to apply the emerging technology.

> The organization will be able to acquire rights to the patents.

> Competitors will not acquire rights to the patents, or will not do so before your organization does.

 ASK the spokesperson from Group 2 to identify the critical assumptions they identified for Situation 2.

LOOK for critical assumptions such as these:

> There actually will be 120 graduates in this emerging field over the next five years, and they will all be willing to work for us.

> Graduates have not already made career commitments (through work-study programs, sponsorships, etc.) to other organizations.

> The public attitude toward genetic research will remain neutral or positive, not turn hostile.

 SUMMARIZE with the following ideas:

> Identifying critical assumptions provides several aids to strategic planning:

>> It helps you identify and quantify risk factors.

>> It identifies areas where the team may need to investigate further before committing to a strategy.

 DISPLAY the overhead transparency, "Critical Success Factors (CSFs)" (on page 185).

FACILITATOR COMMENTARY

 COMMENT with the following ideas:

> The concept of CSFs was introduced by Arthur Andersen and Company in the 1950s, expanded by McKinsey in the 1960s, and described in detail in the literature by John Rockhart at the MIT Sloan School in the late 1970s.

DEFINE critical success factors:

> Critical success factors are the few, high-priority areas which must go just right for the organization to succeed and flourish.

> The organization must manage these factors well to be successful.

> Note the words *critical* and *few*.

> In identifying critical success factors, more is not better.

> Obviously, the vision and mission statement will dictate which few will be critical in a given instance.

But, be aware that CSFs are temporal.

 DISPLAY the overhead transparency, "CSFs—Preparing to Jump" (on page 186).

USE this overhead to illustrate CSFs for a paratrooper to survive a jump.

LIST some CSFs for the paratrooper in this situation on the CSF flipchart:

Pilot skill

The paratrooper's training

Equipment availability and condition

Altitude

Luck.

DISPLAY the overhead transparency, "CSFs— During the Jump" (on page 187).

Group activity

ASK the group to list some CSFs during the jump.

USE the same CSF flipchart, drawing a break line or, using another color pen, record participant comments below the previous list.

LOOK FOR ideas such as these:

The paratrooper's training

Condition of the equipment

Terrain (woodsy? over water?)

Weather conditions (windy? wind in the wrong direction? rain or other visibility factors?).

Group activity

INTRODUCE this group discussion activity with the following comments:

Let's look at a more business-related example of CSFs.

Some critical success factor areas for a nonprofit organization might include:

Funding

Public relations and image

Trained staff with a service orientation.

 ASK the group to suggest some examples for a profit-making organization.

 USE a blank flipchart to record participant comments.

 DISPLAY the overhead transparency, "Example CSFs" (on page 188).

FACILITATOR COMMENTARY

 TRANSITION to the topic of action planning with comments such as:

> *Analysis paralysis* is always a risk in strategic planning.
>
> The planning team can get so involved in visioning, mission statements, critical assumptions, CSFs, and the like, that nothing gets done.
>
> Action planning, our next and final topic, is the solution.

DISPLAY the overhead transparency, "Action Planning" (on page 189).

USE this overhead to define action planning, and to distinguish action plans from simple task lists and "to-do" lists.

Group activity

 WRITE the following statement on a blank flipchart and ask the group to decide whether it is an action plan or a "to-do" list item.

> Determine how many genetic engineering Ph.D. majors are forecast to graduate in the U.S. within the next five years.

SEEK consensus that, while a worthwhile task, this is **not** a real action plan.

ASK what criteria it lacks to qualify as an action plan.

LOOK FOR ideas such as:

> No time frames
>
> No indication of who will carry out the action
>
> No specific commitments to carry out the action
>
> No clear way for management to know (or care) when the action is completed.

DISPLAY the overhead transparency, "Action Planning Approach" (on page 190).

MAKE the following comments:

> This overhead provides an outline that a strategic planning committee should find useful in preparing an action plan document.

DESCRIBE and discuss each item briefly.

DISPLAY the overhead transparency, "The Action Plan" (on page 191).

MAKE the following comments:

This overhead provides a sample worksheet for documenting an action plan. It can be adapted as necessary to fit the needs of the participants' organization and time frame.

DESCRIBE and discuss each item briefly.

CALL attention to the following:

Pay particular note to the box, 5-day/90-day.

A 5-day plan is used immediately after a planning session to gain needed commitments and to energize the implementation of the plan.

A 90-day plan is created and reviewed quarterly with the executive sponsor to maintain momentum and to adjust plans and actions to meet changing requirements.

ASK for questions about action planning.

00:10

Session Wrap-up

FACILITATOR COMMENTARY

THANK the participants for their participation, questions, and ideas.

WRAP UP the session with comments such as:

In this session, we have tried to avoid a rigid, fixed formula for strategic planning.

Instead, we have tried to cause you to see the value of strategic planning, and to think about what is involved.

We have also provided you some useful analytical tools and techniques to get you started with your own strategic planning efforts.

Now all that remains is for *you* and the organization to get started.

> **Procedural note:** *At this point you may wish to ask participants to evaluate your strategic planning session. "Set Two—Session Assessments" (on page 136), provides detailed facilitator instructions and session rating sheets*

Chapter Five

One-day Strategic Planning Workshop

This chapter contains the instructions and materials needed to conduct a one-day (approximately 7-hour) strategic planning workshop. You may use the materials essentially as they appear, or adapt them to the needs of your own organization.

The agenda and methods shown here have been successfully used with small and large businesses, and with the boards of nonprofit organizations, including ASTD chapters, to accomplish actual strategic planning. The purpose of the meeting, as described in this chapter, is to provide an overview of the strategic planning process and to provide key organization leaders a "flavor" for what is involved.

This chapter:

… contains materials you need to plan for and conduct a one-day *strategic planning* meeting. You may use the materials essentially as they appear, or adapt them to the needs of your own organization. It is divided into these parts:

Workshop Purpose and Objectives

Purpose   To lead strategic planning teams through the major steps required to develop and begin implementing an effective strategic plan for their organization.

Objectives   The planning team will be able to:

- Describe the current status of their organization.

- Identify the organization's key stakeholders.

- Identify the organization's key strengths and weaknesses.

- Identify key organizational opportunities and threats to continuing success.

- Determine where the organization ought to be in the future.

- Develop an organizational vision and mission statement.

- Establish and begin implementing an approach for achieving identified target(s).

- Identify Critical Success Factors.

- Develop action plans to begin implementing the team's approach.

Workshop Agenda

One-day Strategic Planning Workshop

	Timing[1]	Start	Stop
"Introduction to the One-day Strategic Planning Workshop " on page 82	00:20	_____	_____
"Phase I: Determine Where We Now Are " on page 85	01:25	_____	_____
"Phase II: Decide Where We Would Like to Be " on page 89	03:10	_____	_____
"Phase III: Establish & Implement Target Approach " on page 100	01:45	_____	_____
"Session Wrap-up" on page 107	00:20	_____	_____

1   Suggested elapsed tim

Facilitation Plan

The following pages provide step-by-step instructions for facilitating a one-day workshop designed to help planning teams develop and begin implementing a strategic plan for their organization.

As you guide participants through the workshop, remember your role as facilitator—to make the planning session happen. Try not to volunteer answers, make decisions for the team, or pass judgment on the decisions the team makes.

00:20

Introduction to the One-day Strategic Planning Workshop

Purposes

Get the workshop off to a positive start by clarifying objectives and mutual roles. Provide a quick overview of the workshop and anticipated outcomes.

FACILITATOR COMMENTARY

 WELCOME participants to the One-day Strategic Planning Workshop. Make these comments:

> You should be pleased to have been selected as a team member for this workshop.

> The ideas you contribute, and the team decisions you make will have a significant impact upon the future of our organization.

> Thank you for committing a day of your time to this important activity.

 DISPLAY the overhead transparency, "One-day Strategic Planning Workshop" on page 193.

USE the overhead to discuss the purpose of the workshop.

 INTRODUCE yourself, explaining your role as facilitator of the meeting.

INTRODUCE any other facilitators (or ask them to introduce themselves).

 ASK each participant to introduce her/himself, addressing the following points:

> Name, title, and responsibility area

> Experience

> Other information of interest.

 REVIEW important logistical details.

> Timing of the meeting

Procedures to follow in the event of an emergency.

 POST the flipchart for the one-day workshop "Agenda" on page 232, at a room location where it can be seen throughout the session.

CHECK OFF the box adjacent to "Introduction" on the flipchart.

COMMENT as follows:

We have now completed session and people introductions.

> **Procedural note:** *You should find this technique useful throughout the session in visually reminding participants where they are in the session and what is coming up next.*

FACILITATOR COMMENTARY

 KICK OFF the workshop with comments such as these:

Organizations that fail to plan long-term often find themselves declining in productivity and profitability, yet with no clear strategy for change.

You could say that, if the organization has no future vision, it is unlikely to change for the better.

Or, as Robert Browning said, "A man's reach should exceed his grasp, or what's a heaven for?"

 DISPLAY the overhead transparency, "Long-term Success Is Within Reach, but Not in Our Grasp" on page 194.

This graphic, based on original work by George Steiner at UCLA and Russell Ackoff at the University of Pennsylvania, illustrates the point.

The bottom, *reference projection* forecasts how things are likely to continue for the organization, if we continue just as we have been doing.

Technology will pass us by. Our competitors will "steal a march" on us. We may even die from complacency.

It takes a healthy dissatisfaction with the present and a vision of the future to avoid this fate.

During the workshop, we will work together to develop a shared vision of our future organization.

We probably will never achieve the entire vision. Our vision is like the uppermost, *wishful projection* on the chart.

But, by going beyond wishful thinking to meaningful strategic planning, we should eventually achieve far greater success than if we plan nothing and do nothing different.

The wishful projection represents the ultimate situation we reach for; the center, planning projection illustrates how we must grasp and achieve parts of the vision along the way, if we are ever to reach our wishful projection.

 DISPLAY the overhead transparency, "Create Organization's Strategic Plan" on page 195.

 MAKE the following points:

Organizations do many types of planning, some formal, some informal. They also use a variety of terms for the types of planning they do. Let's review the planning terms that will be used in this workshop.

EXPLAIN the term *strategic planning.*

Strategic plans are those that define how an organization intends to get from where it is now to where it wants to be in the future.

Strategic plans are the organization's broad, general "road map" for achieving their future vision and mission—the wishful projection we saw on the previous overhead.

Strategic planning typically reflects a relatively long time frame, three to five years (or more).

EXPLAIN the term *tactical planning.*

Tactical plans are used to implement strategic plans.

They are represented by the "planned projection" on the previous overhead.

Tactical plans are measurable, assign responsibilities, and specify completion dates.

They identify major milestones that will help management evaluate progress toward successful implementation of the strategic plan, so that adjustments can be made as required.

Typical tactical plans have believable, relatively short time frames such as 6 to 18 months.

EXPLAIN the term *project planning.*

This is probably the type of planning with which most of us are most familiar.

It is the planning we do day after day, to start projects and see them to completion with a specific, identified set of deliverables.

EXPLAIN the term *action planning.*

Action plans describe short-range courses of action the planning team agree and commit to in preparation for subsequent strategic planning sessions.

 ASK the group if they have questions about distinctions among the planning types.

RESPOND with clarifying comments, as necessary.

 TRANSITION to the strategic planning workshop Phase I:

With these preliminary thoughts in mind, let's get started with our own strategic planning work.

01:25
Phase I:
Determine Where We Now Are

FACILITATOR COMMENTARY

 USE flipchart "Three-phased Approach" on page 233, to overview the three phases of strategic planning.

 EXPLAIN that we will be following the same order to conduct this workshop.

DESCRIBE the Alice in Wonderland story as illustrating the need for having an overall approach:

Lewis Carroll makes an important point about the need for planning an approach in *Alice in Wonderland.* Alice was walking though the woods and suddenly came upon a large tree at a crossroads (paraphrased).

> From nowhere, a Cheshire cat appeared in the tree and asked Alice, "Can I help you?"
>
> Alice said, "Yes, please. I'm lost and need to know which road I should take."
>
> The Cheshire cat asked, "Where are you going?"
>
> Alice said, "Gee, I don't know!"
>
> "Well," said the Cheshire cat, "then it doesn't matter which road you take."

POST the flipchart in a prominent spot, since you will be referring back to it several times throughout the workshop.

 DISPLAY the overhead transparency, "Identify Our Stakeholders, Strengths, Weaknesses, Opportunities, & Threats" on page 196.

 EXPLAIN that these are the defining tasks we will accomplish during Phase I to get a clear picture of where our organization now stands.

DO NOT expect team members to understand the terms yet. Instead:

DESCRIBE briefly, in your own words, what each term means. Give an example that will be relevant to this organization and meaningful to these team members.

USE the space that follows to note examples specific to the participants' organization:

Organization's SWOT Worksheet

Stakeholders (e.g. employees)   _____

A Strength of Our Existing Organization (e.g. customer loyalty)   _____

A Weakness of Our Existing Organization (e.g. product/service quality)   _____

A Potential Opportunity (e.g. entry into a new market or industry)   _____

A Potential Threat (e.g. new competitor)   _____

Procedural note: *There are two versions of the prepared flipchart, "Our Stakeholders (For-profit)" on page 234, or "Our Stakeholders (Nonprofit)" on page 235. Use the appropriate one. Use your "starters" as examples for the following flipcharts. "Starter" examples get the group thinking about other ones.*

 POST the appropriate prepared flipchart "Our Stakeholders..." (referenced above).

 ENTER your "starter" example as the first item.

 CONDUCT a group brainstorming session to identify as complete a list of stakeholders as possible.

RECORD examples on the flipchart.

POST another blank flipchart if necessary.

ALLOW about 5 minutes for this brainstorming activity.

CALL on volunteers to identify whom they believe are the three or four most important stakeholders identified.

ASK for other opinions. Check off a stakeholder each time it is identified. Then:

USE a colored marker to circle the five to ten key stakeholders most mentioned.

POST the flipchart next to the "Three-phased" flipchart.

> **Procedural note:** *If the flipchart is too messy or busy, rewrite a list of the five to ten key stakeholders on a clean flipchart and post it next to the "Three-phased" flipchart.*

DISPLAY the overhead transparency, "SWOT Analysis: Look Internally, Externally" on page 197.

COMMENT as follows:

As a next step in answering the question, "Where are we now?" it is useful to review the organization's current strengths, weaknesses, opportunities, and threats to success.

We refer to this as *SWOT analysis.*

Strengths are areas of value in your organization and among your organization's stakeholders.

One example of an organizational strength is expert staff talent.

Weaknesses are liabilities that exist within the organization, and among the organization's stakeholders.

One example of an organizational weakness is poor organizational communications.

Opportunities represent favorable or advantageous combinations of circumstances that provide the organization with the chance to explore new directions.

One example of an organizational opportunity is an improving business climate.

Threats represent potential dangers from outside the organization that could prevent or inhibit the future success.

Threats may exist both within the organization and among the organization's stakeholders.

One example of an organizational threat is the entry of a competitor.

> **Procedural note:** *For the following activity, you will make better use of time if you divide up the discussion of Strengths, Weaknesses, Opportunities, and Threats among either two or four small groups. There should be at least three people in each group.*

Small group activity

 DIVIDE the group into small groups.

 POST the following flipcharts near the small groups you have identified.

"Our Organization's Strengths" on page 236

"Our Organization's Weaknesses" on page 237

"Our Organization's Opportunities" on page 238

"Our Organization's Threats" on page 239.

 INTRODUCE each flipchart by writing a pertinent "starter" example on it.

ASSIGN one (or two) flipcharts to each group.

ASK the groups to discuss organizational-specific examples relate to the flipchart(s) they have been assigned.

 DIRECT each table group to spend 10 to 15 minutes formulating examples.

ASK them to record their ideas on the appropriate flipchart(s).

MOVE around the room observing progress. Do not offer suggestions, but feel free to ask leading questions if any group appears to be unproductive.

Group activity

 RECONVENE the full group after 15 minutes, or as soon as productivity begins to lag.

 CALL ON each group to present ideas.

ASK clarifying questions if necessary. After each group presents findings,

ASK other group members if they wish to add ideas.

RECORD additional, productive ideas on the appropriate flipchart.

POST the flipcharts prominently, so the group will be able to refer to them during phases II and III.

 TRANSITION to Phase II, with your own comments or comments such as the following:

> This completes our Phase I activities.
>
> What we have done is to get a clearer, more focused picture of our organization as it now exists.

> **Procedural note:** *Use the posted flipcharts to draw attention to particularly significant findings about the organization's current status.*

DIRECT attention to the flipchart, "Three-phased Approach" that you posted at the beginning of this phase.

CHECK OFF the Phase I box with a colored marker to indicate we have completed Phase I and are ready to begin Phase II.

COMMENT as follows:

In the next phase of our strategic planning process, we will begin considering what our organization might become.

03:10

Phase II:
Decide Where We Would Like to Be

FACILITATOR COMMENTARY

REFER to the posted flipchart, "Three-phased Approach" to introduce Phase II.

DISPLAY the overhead transparency, "Create a Vision, Write Mission Statement" on page 198.

INTRODUCE Phase II using the two topics of this overhead.

MAKE the following points to overview the process.

> During this session we will create a first draft vision and mission statement.
>
> After the workshop, you, the core planning team, will want to share your preliminary vision and mission statement with the key stakeholders you have identified.
>
> You should anticipate suggested changes!

It will be necessary to revise your vision and mission statement repeatedly until it is shared by all key stakeholders. This is one way to get them to "buy into" your strategic plan.

Once you have obtained that buy-in, your team will be ready to begin determining the steps necessary to achieve the mission.

 DISPLAY the overhead transparency, "To Create a Vision, Change Your Frame of Reference" on page 199.

FACILITATOR COMMENTARY

 INTRODUCE the visioning exercise, using this overhead.

One of our objectives for Phase II is to develop a joint vision of what the organization *could* be.

This is not an easy way of thinking for most us. We tend to focus on today's problems, realities, and constraints.

We tend to make our day-to-day decisions on the basis of past successes and failures.

A useful technique to get us out of that mode of thinking is to place ourselves in the future and look back to see how we must have gotten there.

 DISPLAY the overhead transparency, "Visioning Exercises Create a View of Future Success" on page 200.

 USE this overhead to begin focusing the team on the visioning task.

 DISPLAY the overhead transparency "To Be Creative, We Must Act Roles," (1) or (2), page 201 or page 202.

 ASK if anyone is familiar with Van Oech. Allow volunteers to comment on what they have read or presentations they have attended.

 INTRODUCE others on the team to Van Oech and his views on how to think creatively.

In his book, *A Whack on the Side of the Head*, Van Oech suggested ways to develop new ideas through play.

In a more recent book, *A Kick in the Seat of the Pants*, Van Oech continues the play technique, but introduces the concepts of *explorer, artist, judge,* and *warrior*.

Each of these individuals has a different role in being creative. In fact, we must borrow from each of their techniques.

DISCUSS the role of the explorer:

Creative thinking is not devoid of facts, concepts, experiences.

Like an explorer, it is necessary to put forth the effort to look at new things, gain new experiences, and also look at old things in new ways.

During the course of searching, explorers look for unusual patterns, unanticipated relationships, and contrary-to-logic notions.

In Phase I, you began fulfilling the explorer role.

DISCUSS the role of the artist:

With this pile of new ideas and notions, you have to shift gears, and release the artist within yourself.

Like the artist, you need to look for patterns.

You rearrange the pile, look at things backwards, ask yourself "What if" questions, look for hidden similarities and analogies among what are seemingly utterly different concepts and clusters of facts.

Having done so, you are likely to come up with a new idea or two.

You do not care, as artist, whether your new ideas seem harebrained or practical to others.

DISCUSS the role of the judge:

Time to change hats again (or maybe robes)!

As judge, you critically evaluate your new ideas. You ask yourself questions such as:

Does this idea have merit?

If it could be achieved, would the results be worthwhile for the organization?

Could I sell this idea to our stakeholders? Are there drawbacks?

Is the timing right?

Ultimately, you make a decision, even if it is a gut decision.

DISCUSS the role of the warrior:

Warriors get things done.

They defend new ideas against ideas competing for funds and resources.

Warriors are objective oriented; they view obstacles as a challenge, nor a reason to stop trying.

MAKE the following points.

During Phase I, we worked in an explorer role.

We are now going to shift to the artist role.

We will revisit the judge and warrior later, so put them on the sidelines for now.

Group activity

DISPLAY the overhead transparency, "Before Creating Our Vision, We Must Be in a Creative Mood" on page 203.

EXPLAIN that the group is going to participate in a creative thinking exercise.

ASK anyone who is already familiar with this exercise NOT to reveal the answer, but instead, to look for solutions other than the one they already know.

DESCRIBE the rules:

In this apparently random row of letters is a hidden word.

> You can find it by crossing out six letters.
>
> To succeed, you must use non-conventional thinking.
>
> Hold up your hand when you believe you have found the word, but don't reveal the solution to others.

ASK if there are questions about the rules. Respond as necessary.

ALLOW about five minutes, or until several people appear to have the solution.

CALL on the first person to hold his/her hand up to reveal the solution.

> **Procedural note:** *One solution to this puzzle is to think of the phrase, "six letters" not numerically but as the two words "six" and "letters." When these two words are crossed out, the word "BANANA" remains.*
>
> *A second solution is to eliminate all incidences of the **first** six letters. The first six letters are B S A I N and X. A, N, and S occur twice. When they are removed, the word "LETTER" remains.*

MAKE NOTE of the following ideas:

> This demonstrates an important lesson. Generally people stop when they find an answer to a puzzle.
>
> The artist role in creativity demands more—you must keep looking for additional answers and solutions.

Optional group activity

 DISPLAY the overhead transparency, "Visioning Exercises Create a View of Future Success" on page 200.

 USE the overhead to reinforce the following process. Then:

 EXPLAIN that, to give participants a flavor for the visioning technique, you are going to ask them to participate in a brief visioning exercise.

 READ the following visioning instructions to the participants.

Pause briefly (15 to 20 seconds) between each statement to allow participants to begin to relax.

Put all your materials aside.

Make yourself comfortable in your chair.

Close your eyes if you wish [long pause].

It is now four to six years in the future.

Your organization has just been selected to receive the Twenty-first Century Award, the most prestigious citation given any national enterprise.

Since you were a key player in the efforts that led to your organization's success, you have been selected to appear before a joint session of your country's legislative body.

You are sitting in the anteroom of the legislative hall, awaiting the beginning of the session in which you will accept your organization's award from the country's highest government official.

> You have just learned from a key aide that, in addition to receiving the award for your organization, you will also be asked to briefly describe what occurred in your organization over the past five years that has led to this moment.
>
> > How does the organization now differ from what it was four years ago?
> >
> > What positive changes have occurred?
> >
> > How were they achieved?
> >
> > Did technological developments contribute to these changes?
> >
> > You took advantage of what other opportunities, if any?
>
> You review your notes and begin collecting your thoughts.

ASK the participants to take from three to five minutes thinking about what they would say.

REMIND them that, since this is a visioning exercise, they are free to make any assumptions they wish. After five minutes,

ASK for several volunteers to present their visions.

WRAP UP the exercise with comments such as:

> Did you notice how the visioning technique of looking back from the future allowed you to open up your mind to additional possibilities?
>
> You were no longer confined in your thinking to current realities and constraints.

> **Procedural note:** *This is a good place in the workshop to take a break, before moving on to the team's own organizational visioning task.*

Organizational Visioning Activity

FACILITATOR COMMENTARY

 DISPLAY the overhead transparency, "Visioning Exercises Involve Thinking About the Future and Picturing Results," on page 204.

 EXPLAIN the following points:

> We are now going to participate in developing a shared vision for our own organization.

We will follow the same basic procedure we used during the visioning exercise, but the questions will be somewhat different.

Procedural note: *The following instructions and script will fit most situations. However, you should adapt them as necessary to fit the circumstances of the organization.*

Remember to turn off the overhead projector and minimize distractions.

 READ the following visioning instructions to the participants.

Pause briefly (15 to 20 seconds) between each statement to allow participants to relax and contemplate their ideas.

- Put all your materials aside.

- Make yourself comfortable in your chair.

- Close your eyes if you wish [long pause].

- It is now four years today.

- Four years ago, we were viewed in the press as an organization stagnating in flat growth. Now, business sections of newspapers across the U.S. and abroad are writing about our amazing turnaround.

- In fact, the Corporation for Public Broadcasting has called and asked to interview someone on the *Nightly Business Report*.

- You have been asked to help organize the key messages that should be included in the interview. You will be providing input directly to the program's producer and want to make sure the program provides a balanced perspective on the changes your organization has experienced.

  - *How does the organization now differ from what it was four years ago?*
  - *What positive changes have occurred?*
  - *How were they achieved?*
  - *Did technological developments contribute to these changes?*
  - *What other opportunities, if any, did you take advantage of?*

ALLOW individuals 15 minutes to jot down ideas and develop a response. After 15 minutes (or after most people appear to have finished):

ASK volunteers to present their ideas to the full group.

RECORD ideas on blank flipcharts.

POST flipcharts where planning team members will be able to refer to them throughout the remainder of the workshop.

FACILITATOR COMMENTARY

INTRODUCE the following ideas in moving to the next part of Phase II, Developing a Mission Statement.

> We now have developed several elements of the future vision of our organization.
>
> One way of solidifying that vision is to create an organizational mission statement that we can all buy into—at least provisionally.
>
> It will be important, after this workshop is over, to share our vision and mission statement with the key stakeholders we identified during Phase I.
>
> We should all anticipate further refinements in the vision and mission statement we develop today. Strategic planning is an iterative process.

DISPLAY the overhead transparency, "A Mission Statement Describes the Organization's Long-term Direction" on page 205.

DESCRIBE the value and purpose(s) of a mission statement using this overhead.

REMIND the group to look over their list of stakeholders.

ASK if there are stakeholders that will be affected by the team's new vision.

ASK if **new** stakeholders should be added to the organizational stakeholders flipchart, given the team's new vision.

ADD any new stakeholder suggestions to the flipchart page.

ASK what existing or new stakeholder needs the new vision will better satisfy.

RECORD key ideas on a blank flipchart page.

POST the flipchart where the group can reflect back on them as they develop their mission statement.

DISPLAY the overhead transparency, "No One Correct Mission Statement Style" on page 206.

MAKE the following comments.

> This overhead shows some typical mission statements.
>
> Some are brief, some are long.

In general, the more succinct and inclusive the better (although those can be conflicting goals).

The last mission statement is that of ISPI, a professional, nonprofit organization.

 DISPLAY the overhead transparency, "Mission Statement Includes Vision, Measurement, Theme" on page 207.

 COMMENT with the following ideas:

One design for structuring a mission statement comes from Peter Drucker and Russell Ackoff.

They suggest that, at a minimum, a mission statement should encompass the organization's vision, a way of measuring or assessing the achievement of that mission, and a unique organizational theme.

Mission Statement Development Activity

 DIVIDE the group into two or four small groups depending on the planning team size. Avoid groups of fewer than three.

 DISPLAY the overhead transparency, "Questions Help Us Form Mission Statement" on page 208.

ASK the groups to use this overhead as a structural device to formulate draft mission statements for the organization.

 MAKE the following points:

Use this structure to help you develop your first draft of a mission statement for the organization.

If, later, you prefer another approach, you can use it to refine this initial effort.

Procedural note: *There are two versions of the prepared flipchart, "Mission Statement (For-profit)" on page 240, and "Mission Statement (Nonprofit)" on page 241.*

Each flipchart shows a mission statement from an organization, which can serve as a model or be rejected. Use the prepared flipchart appropriate for your organization.

 POST the appropriate flipchart headed "Mission Statement..."

ALLOW the team time to read the example mission statement.

POINT out its brevity.

POINT out its focus on stakeholder values.

ASK each group to assign a group spokesperson.

ASK each group to begin formulating draft mission statements for the organization.

EXPLAIN the following points:

> You will have 45 minutes to discuss the contents of your mission statement and prepare a draft statement.
>
> When your table group is in reasonable agreement, write your draft on a blank flipchart page (or blank overhead transparency).
>
> I will all time in 35 minutes. At that point, each table group should put something on paper, even if there is not complete group consensus.

ASK for and answer any procedural questions.

INSTRUCT the groups to begin.

MONITOR progress, but do not intervene unless absolutely necessary.

ANNOUNCE "ten minutes remaining," after 35 minutes have elapsed. Tell groups to begin recording their draft mission statements.

CALL ON a spokesperson from each group to present a draft mission statement.

CONDUCT a discussion to identify the most acceptable components of each draft mission statement.

RECORD key components of desirable mission statements on a blank flipchart.

ALLOW about ten minutes for final suggestions and the creation of a final draft mission statement.

Procedural note: *This is a good point for another brief break.*

During the break, transcribe the final draft mission statement onto the prepared flipchart, "Our Mission Statement" on page 243.

You may want to enlist the assistance of some of the people who recorded the draft mission statements.

POST the prepared flipchart with the transcribed, final draft mission statement in a prominent place in the room.

 RECONVENE the workshop.

ASK the team to review the final draft mission statement.

ADJUST as required to gain consensus or, that failing, list "establishing the achievement of consensus" as a future action item.

CONCLUDE Phase II with comments such as:

> You have now developed a first draft mission statement. That is a major step toward a new strategic direction for the organization.

> After the workshop, it will be important to review your draft mission statement with as many key stakeholders as you can, and solicit their ideas.

> They will suggest refinements that will make your mission statement even more focused and realistic.

 DIRECT attention to the prepared flipchart, "Three-phased Approach" on page 233, that you posted at the beginning of this workshop.

CHECK OFF the Phase II box with a colored marker to indicate we have completed Phase II and are ready to begin Phase III.

 TRANSITION to Phase III with comments such as:

> Any mission statement is useless unless there is a plan to implement the vision and mission statement.

> We will begin that task in Phase III.

01:45

Phase III:
Establish & Implement Target Approach

FACILITATOR COMMENTARY

 REFER TO THE POSTED flipchart, "Three-phased Approach," to introduce Phase III.

EXPLAIN that each team is now going to begin creating a strategy to realize the mission statement they created during the last phase of the workshop.

 DISPLAY the overhead transparency, "Identify Opportunities, CSFs, Critical Assumptions" on page 209.

EXPLAIN that to get started, you would like to review some key terms and concepts.

REVIEW each term on this overhead, and/or ask for volunteers to explain each term and provide an example relevant to their organization and strategic plan.

ASK if anyone has an opinion on why *milestones* and *outcomes* are listed on the overhead before *activities*.

LOOK FOR response(s) expressing ideas such as:

> It is easy to jump from action plans to activities, without carefully considering what results we want to see and accomplish.

> It is a matter of intellectual discipline.

> By forcing ourselves to focus on milestones and outcomes first, we are more likely to define activities with useful results.

 ASK the group if any more clarification of these terms is needed.

RESPOND as necessary.

Opportunity Identification Activity

> **Procedural note:** *Be sure flipcharts from previous activities (SWOT analysis, mission statement, etc.) are posted and visible.*

FACILITATOR COMMENTARY

 INTRODUCE the activity with these comments:

> With this activity, your goal is to identify opportunities that will help your organization accomplish the new mission you previously identified.

DEFINE "opportunity" as:

> **Opportunity:** *Favorable or advantageous combinations of circumstances that provide the chance to explore new directions.*

OVERVIEW the steps:

> Working as a full group, we will go through these steps:
>
> First, we'll look at the previous work we have done—SWOT analysis and mission statement—to assemble ideas.
>
> Then, we'll brainstorm as complete a list of potential opportunities as possible, while withholding judgment as to the relative worth of each idea.
>
> Then, we'll strive to reach consensus regarding the five to six opportunity ideas which have the most merit—the ones with the greatest likelihood of return for the organization.

REFER participants to the flipcharts reflecting work to this point, particularly SWOT analysis and mission statement.

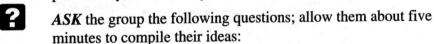 *ASK* the group the following questions; allow them about five minutes to compile their ideas:

> Which of the opportunities identified during our SWOT analysis still appear to support the mission we have since defined?
>
> What new opportunities can you think of?

 POST the flipchart "Our Best Opportunities" on page 242.

> **Procedural note:** *Allow about five minutes for participants to develop ideas.*
>
> *Then, ask for volunteers (or call on individuals) to offer their suggestions.*
>
> *Discourage critiques by reminding participants that this is a brainstorming session.*
>
> *Encourage participants to build on ideas others suggest.*
>
> *Record ideas on the posted, prepared flipchart. Use additional blank flipchart pages if necessary.*

RECORD participant opportunity suggestions on the flipchart.

ASK participants if they need clarification on any opportunities listed.

ASK the participant who contributed the questioned opportunity to elaborate.

> **Procedural note:** *Since you will be asking participants to leave their seats for the following prioritization activity, this may be an opportune time to build in a break.*
>
> *Ask participants to record their preferences, then go on break.*

 COMMENT as follows:

Now I want each of you to come up and place a check mark by the three opportunities on the flipchart(s) you feel have most merit or likelihood of success.

Check off no more than three.

> **Procedural note:** *An alternative to having participants check off opportunities is to issue each of them three colored stick-on dots or stars to place next to the opportunities they prefer.*
>
> *When the group is finished, identify the five or six opportunities with the most votes.*

 REVIEW the five to six opportunities the group has identified as most viable.

CONCLUDE the activity with the following:

We will revisit these opportunities throughout the remainder of our workshop.

> **Procedural note:** *Given sufficient time, you might assign one or two of the opportunities identified to subgroups and have them base the final activities— CSFs, critical assumptions, and action plans—on the opportunities they have been assigned.*
>
> *However, since this is only a one-day workshop, the remainder of the instructions ask the group to focus on CSFs, critical assumptions, and action plans in the context of the mission statement defined earlier.*
>
> *If a group has identified an opportunity with broad consensus, you may want to structure the balance of the workshop on that one opportunity, rather than on their broad mission statement.*

Small group activity

 DISPLAY the overhead transparency, "Identify CSFs for Vision, Mission Statements" on page 210.

 POST copies of the flipchart, "Our Critical Success Factors" on page 244, near each group's work area.

FACILITATOR COMMENTARY

 INTRODUCE the critical success factors (CSF) activity with comments such as:

> Each group is now going to take a few minutes to reflect on and identify the critical success factors underlying the vision components and the final draft mission statement we developed during the last phase of the workshop.

> When you get started, you should first review the vision components and final draft mission statement.

> Then, place yourself mentally into the future and assume your mission statement has been achieved. Think about what it was that got you there.

> Identify the factors that must have been critical to this achievement. "What had to have happened just right to be where you are now?"

> Take a few minutes to brainstorm, without passing judgment. You will have about 15 minutes.

> At the end of that time, I will ask you to begin recording your CSFs on the flipcharts next to your group's work area.

 ALLOW 15 minutes for groups to brainstorm. Then ask them to record the CSFs they have agreed upon on a blank flipchart or blank overhead transparency.

Group activity

 ASK for groups to present their CSFs and explain the rationale behind each CSF. When each group completes its presentation.

POLL the full group to pick three to six CSFs all agree are critical.

 CONCLUDE the activity with a comment such as:

> Critical success factors are just that, critical to the success of your strategic plan.

Procedural note: *Consensus on three to six CSFs at this point is critical before moving ahead. Neither the group nor the organization can manage too many CSFs at the same time.*

REINTRODUCE the concept of critical assumptions.

> You will not achieve desired success unless you also identify the critical assumptions you have made before moving on.

ASK for a volunteer to explain and give an example of a critical assumption. Verify the example.

> **Procedural note:** *As an alternative to asking for a volunteer, you may want to offer these examples:*
>
> *"The economy will improve 6.2% in the next 12 months."*
>
> *"People with all the critical skills needed are available and can be hired."*

Group activity

POST flipchart "Our Critical Assumptions" on page 245.

ASK for volunteers to identify critical assumptions for the CSFs the group has selected as the three to six most critical.

RECORD each critical assumption that the group seems largely to agree upon on the flipchart.

ALLOW about five minutes, or until the group runs out of ideas.

DISPLAY the overhead transparency, "Now You Need an Action Plan" on page 211.

> **Procedural note:** *Before beginning this activity, locate the overhead, "The Action Plan" on page 213, and make approximately five print copies per participant.*

Small group activity

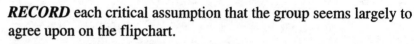

FACILITATOR COMMENTARY

REVISIT the definition of action plan.

DISPLAY the overhead transparency, "Create Action Plan, Gain Commitment" on page 212.

DIVIDE CSFs and *critical assumptions* among the groups.

> **Procedural note:** *Allow groups to reorganize as necessary to have participants work on issues or opportunities most important to them.*

ASK each group to focus on key areas they have interest in.

OVERVIEW this group activity using the overhead.

EMPHASIZE the importance of defining outcomes first.

COMMENT that this is the one activity most critical to the success of their strategic plan. Therefore, the groups should commit significant time and effort.

 DISPLAY the overhead transparency, "The Action Plan" on page 213.

 USE this overhead to explain the components of the action plan.

> **Procedural note:** *Distribute print copies of the "Action Plan" overhead to each group.*

 POST a copy of the flipchart "Action Plan" on page 246 near each group's work area.

 EXPLAIN that the groups will have 45 minutes to develop their action plans. You will remain available to assist and answer questions, but each group must take ownership of their plans.

REMIND groups (if necessary) to enter their action plans on the flipchart organizer, at least 15 minutes before you plan to resume the full session.

> **Procedural note:** *Allow groups as much time as possible during the remainder of the afternoon, but set a firm cut-off that will leave sufficient time to debrief each group and conclude the workshop.*

Group activity   **FACILITATOR COMMENTARY**

 RECONVENE the full group.

 DEBRIEF each group by asking them to present their action plans.

ASK other groups to make constructive suggestions about how the presenting group's action plan might be enhanced.

REPEAT this activity with each group.

DIRECT attention to the flipchart, "Three-phased Approach" on page 233, that you posted at the beginning of this workshop.

CHECK OFF the Phase III box with a colored marker to indicate we have completed all three phases.

00:20

Session Wrap-up

 *DISPLAY* the overhead transparency, "Help Organization Reach Its Vision, Mission" on page 214, or "Now We Must Commit to Meeting the Vision, Mission" on page 215.

FACILITATOR COMMENTARY

 CONCLUDE the workshop with comments such as:

Your planning group now has a first draft of a strategic plan for your organization.

You have a vision, a mission statement, CSFs, critical assumptions, and action plans to implement your strategic plan.

You still have to sell your strategic plan to all the stakeholders you've identified.

You still have to make it all happen, but since you know where you are going, and have plans for getting there, you are likely to succeed.

Procedural note: *At this point you may wish to have participants evaluate their strategic planning session.*

The assessments chapter of this book provides detailed facilitator instructions.

Chapter Six:

Strategic Planning Activities

Here are some activities related to strategic planning that you should find useful, either to hone your own skills and understanding of underlying concepts, or to use with strategic planning groups within your organization.

This Chapter

...provides activities. Each activity contains:

    Brief introductory comments
    A set of instructions for carrying out the activity
    Activity worksheets to be filled in

Use these materials by:

    Keying them into your word processing system, as published
    Customizing them to suit your needs
    Or, photocopying them directly from this book.

Identify Stakeholders

In any organization, certain people (or groups) have vested interests in, or can significantly influence the success of the organization. For an organization to succeed, key stakeholders must be identified early.

This is particularly true in strategic planning, since stakeholders can either endorse and support the strategic plan or create roadblocks to its success.

Examples of Stakeholders

Stakeholders may be either individuals or groups. Stakeholders are almost never exactly the same for any two organizations. For example, suppose a manufacturing firm is creating a strategic plan. A few key stakeholders might include:

> Director of manufacturing
>
> Director of research and development
>
> Potential buyers of the products (customers)
>
> Distributors.

Now, suppose a professional society such as ASTD is creating a strategic plan. Stakeholders in this effort might include:

> Training departments and companies
>
> Companies in a particular geographic area
>
> Individuals new to the field of training (both students and employees who have been moved into a training or HRD position)
>
> Current members (you don't want to alienate them).

In each situation you can probably list many others.

Activity instructions

Stakeholder Identification Worksheet

Identify the key stakeholders for the current phase of your strategic (or other project) plan, and assign them by relative level of importance.

Stakeholder Identification Worksheet

Highly Important

_____

_____

_____

_____

_____

_____

_____

Moderately Important

_____

_____

_____

_____

_____

_____

_____

Less Important

_____

_____

_____

_____

_____

_____

_____

Identify SWOT: *Strengths, Weaknesses, Opportunities, Threats*

An important activity when you are trying to define the current status of your organization is to perform a *SWOT analysis*. What are your group's current, major *strengths, weaknesses*? What are its potential *opportunities* and *threats?*

	Internal	External
+	Strengths	Opportunities
−	Weaknesses	Threats

Here is a single example of each, to get you started:

  Strength—Core of committed employees

  Weakness—Lack of an organizational research arm

  Opportunity—Unfilled demand for product or service

  Threat—New entries into the business or professional activity.

SWOT Identification Worksheet

Activity instructions

Use the following questions to do a SWOT analysis of your organization's current status:

  What are our *strengths*?

  What are our *weaknesses*?

  What *opportunities* now exist (or are likely to soon exist) that we should be taking advantage of?

  What are current (or looming) *threats* to our continuing success?

SWOT Identification Worksheet

Strengths

_____
_____
_____
_____
_____
_____
_____
_____
_____

Opportunities

_____
_____
_____
_____
_____
_____
_____
_____
_____

Weaknesses

_____
_____
_____
_____
_____
_____
_____
_____
_____

Threats

_____
_____
_____
_____
_____
_____
_____
_____
_____

Set the Vision

A core element of strategic planning is the development of a vision of what the organization *can* and *should* be.

> **Vision:** *A mental picture of what the organization should look like in the future and how it will feel to interact with its stakeholders.*

Going beyond that narrow definition, the process of visioning can lead to a valuable set of shared ideas. This shared vision can help lead an organization toward the development of a specific, detailed mission statement. Developing a shared vision also helps the organization's strategic planning team later in the strategic planning process as they identify and prioritize opportunities.

The following visioning instructions copy those used in the *One-day Strategic Planning Workshop* presented elsewhere in this book. Feel free to adapt them to your organization's needs.

Organizational Visioning Activity Instructions

Activity instructions

During this activity, participants in a group will develop a shared vision for their organization.

> **Procedural note:** *The following instructions and script will fit most situations. However, you should adapt them as necessary to fit the circumstances of your organization.*

Read the following visioning instructions to the participants.

Pause briefly (15 to 20 seconds) between each statement to allow participants to relax and contemplate their ideas.

Put all your materials aside.

Make yourself comfortable in your chair.

Close your eyes if you wish [long pause].

It is now four years from today.

Four years ago, we were viewed in the press as an organization in a state of flux. Now, our organization is being featured in the business section of newspapers across the U.S. and abroad for our amazing results.

In fact, we have been notified by the Corporation for Public Broadcasting that they would like to do an interview feature on *The Nightly Business Report.*

You have been asked to help organize the key messages that should be included in the interview. You will be providing input directly to the program's producer and want to make sure that the program provides a balanced perspective on the changes your organization has experienced.

How does the organization now differ from what it was four years ago?

What positive changes have occurred?

How were they achieved?

Did technological developments contribute to these changes?

What other opportunities, if any, did you take advantage of?

After reading the script, allow individuals 15 minutes to develop a response. After 15 minutes (or after most people appear to have finished):

Ask volunteers to present their ideas to the full group.

Record ideas on blank flipcharts.

Organizational Visioning Activity Worksheet

Vision Responses   *Jot down your responses to the questions here*

_____

_____

_____

_____

_____

_____

_____

_____

_____

_____

_____

_____

_____

_____

_____

_____

_____

_____

_____

Establish the Mission

The mission statement can be thought of as a formal statement of how the strategic planning team believes the organization should go about realizing its shared vision.

> **Mission:** *A formal statement describing the future direction of the organization that is consistent with the values, goals, and objectives of the stakeholders as a group.*

There is no pat formula for a mission statement—so long as it meets the requirements identified in the mission definition above. However, Peter Drucker and Russell Ackhoff suggest including the following elements:

Vision

What should we be doing?

What should be the results?

Measurement

To what standard should we perform our mission?

Theme

How should the accomplishment of this mission benefit our key stakeholders?

As you carry out this activity, you should include these elements.

Mission Identification Worksheet

Activity instructions

Review your (or your team's) vision statement. Then respond to the worksheet questions.

> **Note:** *This activity requires intensive thought and concentration. Take the time required to do a thorough job, even if you are only able to address part of your total vision.*

Mission Identification Worksheet

What should we be doing, and what should the results be?

_____
_____
_____
_____
_____
_____
_____

What standards should we use?

_____
_____
_____
_____
_____
_____
_____
_____

How should the accomplishment of this mission benefit our key stakeholders?

_____
_____
_____
_____
_____
_____
_____

Identify Opportunities

With this activity, your goal is to identify opportunities that will help your organization accomplish the new mission you previously identified.

> **Opportunity:** *Favorable or advantageous combinations of circumstances that provide the chance to explore new directions.*

Whether you are working alone or as a group on this activity, you should take it in two steps:

Brainstorm as complete a list of ideas as possible, while withholding judgment as to the relative worth of each idea.

Then, try to reach a decision (individual or group) regarding the five to six ideas which have the most merit—the ones with the greatest likelihood of return for the organization.

Opportunity Identification Worksheet

Activity instructions

First develop responses to these questions:

Which of the opportunities identified during the SWOT analysis still appear to support the defined mission?

What new opportunities can you think of?

When you have compiled your list, check off the five or six opportunities which you believe (or the group agrees) offer the most potential.

Opportunity Identification Worksheet

Opportunity	Highest Potential
_____	_____
_____	_____
_____	_____
_____	_____
_____	_____
_____	_____
_____	_____
_____	_____
_____	_____
_____	_____
_____	_____
_____	_____
_____	_____
_____	_____
_____	_____
_____	_____
_____	_____
_____	_____

Identify CSFs/Critical Assumptions:
Critical Success Factors, Critical Assumptions

Having identified opportunities is not enough. Certain things must occur (or **not** occur) if the opportunity is to be realized. In this activity, you (or the team) will identify the factors critical to success, along with the assumptions upon which you are basing your plans.

> **Critical Success Factors (CSFs)** : *The few, high-priority areas the organization must manage to be successful.*
>
> **Critical Assumptions** : *The few, key assumptions on which the organization is basing its plans.*

For the purposes of this activity, you are asked to work on only three of the opportunities you delineated in the previous activity. Of course, if time permits, you may want to do more.

Activity instructions

CSF/Critical Assumptions ID Worksheet

Use these worksheets to record your responses to the following questions:

What is the opportunity being addressed?

What few things **must** go right for us to achieve this opportunity.

What basic, underlying assumptions are we making?

CSF/Critical Assumptions ID Worksheet (1)

Description of Opportunity One

_____

_____

Critical Success Factors

_____

_____

_____

_____

_____

_____

_____

_____

Critical Assumptions

_____

_____

_____

_____

_____

_____

_____

_____

CSF/Critical Assumptions ID Worksheet (2)

Description of Opportunity Two

_____

_____

Critical Success Factors

_____

_____

_____

_____

_____

_____

_____

_____

Critical Assumptions

_____

_____

_____

_____

_____

_____

_____

_____

_____

CSF/Critical Assumptions ID Worksheet (3)

Description of Opportunity Three

_____

_____

Critical Success Factors

_____

_____

_____

_____

_____

_____

_____

_____

Critical Assumptions

_____

_____

_____

_____

_____

_____

_____

_____

Develop Action Plans

In this activity, you will develop an action plan to accomplish at least two of the opportunities you have identified. You will probably want to select from those for which you developed CSFs and critical assumptions, since those are probably best thought out.

Try to keep in mind that we are thinking of action plans in support of your organization's strategic plan, not the types of project planning with which you may be more familiar. Let's revisit some definitions:

Action Plans: Short-range plans developed to identify activities, outcomes, responsible parties, and target dates needed to help measure the success of achieving the organization's mission, goals, and objectives

Outcomes: The observable results of activities

Activities: Actions that result in, or contribute to, an outcome

Here is an example which is a portion of an action plan prepared by a small software manufacturer whose vision is to be recognized as the leading provider of a specialized financial software system. The software company has identified standard trade shows as one opportunity.

Description of Opportunity
Exhibit in at least one trade show per national region (East Coast, Central, West Coast) during the next fiscal year.

Action Planning Worksheet

Activity instructions

Use the "Example Action Plan (Fragment)" below to see how to structure your action plan.

Photocopy the "Action Planning Worksheet" on page 127 as needed to create additional action plans.

Example Action Plan (Fragment)

Outcome	By Whom	By When	Activity
Overall planning complete	H. Wells	June 30	Identify trade show locations, entry fees, facilities blueprints; local lodging accommodations
Exhibit booth built	L. Hagenbaum	Aug 30	Plan/design booth
			Verify conformance with size/height requirements of **all** locations
			Select construction subcontractor

Action Planning Worksheet

Description of Opportunity Number _____

_____

_____

_____

Action Plan

Outcome	By Whom	By When	Activity

Chapter Seven:

Assessments

Here are three sets of assessment tools:

This Chapter

...provides these assessment tools:

"Set One—Preparation Assessments" on page 130, provides several tools to use in preparation for the strategic planning session. *This is for your use, not participants* .

"Set Two—Session Assessments" on page 136, helps participants evaluate the worth of a strategic planning session. Feedback from these should be useful in streamlining future sessions.

"Set Three—Results, Progress Assessments" on page 143, helps you and the executive sponsor evaluate progress and redirect efforts, as necessary. *This set is not for participants.*

Bear in mind that each of the assessment tools in this sourcebook is, in itself, a strategic planning tool. You should think of these sessions not as *training* but tools to help organizations define and achieve their strategic goals and objectives. Thus, the assessment tools you will find here are somewhat different from those used for more traditional training programs.

You can use the assessments in any of these ways:

Key them into your own word processing system, as published

Or customize them to suit your specific needs

Photocopy the masters you need from this book.

Set One— *Preparation Assessments*

This set contains three assessment tools:

"Assess the Executive Sponsor's Readiness for Change" on page 130

"Assess Existing Mission Statements" on page 131

"Assess Potential Members of Strategic Planning Team" on page 133.

Use these tools to help prepare for your strategic planning session(s).

Assess the Executive Sponsor's Readiness for Change

Strategic planning entails a significant investment in the time of high-level resources. Implementing the changes that almost inevitably result from strategic planning will entail strong executive backing and, usually, monetary investments.

For your strategic planning efforts to succeed, the executive sponsor must recognize these realities. If he/she does not, strategic planning should probably be deferred until the need for change is recognized and accepted at the executive level.

The following assessment tool contains a series of questions you should be asking yourself and, when in doubt, verifying with the executive sponsor. The tool identifies some significant issues you need to resolve before agreeing to head up a strategic planning session.

> **NOTE:** *This assessment tool is not intended as a checklist to be used in the executive sponsor's presence, but as a thought-stimulator for your meetings and discussions with the executive sponsor in preparation for conducting a strategic planning session.*

The Executive Sponsor is Probably Ready for Organizational Change if He/She:

❑   Has expressed concern about or dissatisfaction with the current performance and direction of the organization.

❑   Has set reasonable targets and goals for change.

❑   Has a grasp of the processes of strategic planning.

❑   Has expressed a willingness to invest time and high-level resources.

❑   Is willing to invest your time—relieving you of conflicting responsibilities.

❑   Has expressed a willingness to try out new ideas and directions, even if they are not totally congruent with his/her current thoughts.

❑   Is willing to commit his/her personal attention to strategic planning activities, throughout the process.

❑   Is willing to commit to monitoring strategic planning progress.

❑   Is willing to personally review and approve action plans the strategic planning team recommends, and to fund the action plans he/she approves.

❑   Understands the risks of failure to support strategic planning over the long-haul.

Assess Existing Mission Statements

When preparing for your strategic planning session, you may discover that the organization already has a mission statement. (There may have been earlier strategic planning sessions or other mission statement development efforts.) If so, someone in your strategic planning session is bound to ask, "What is wrong with the mission statement we already have?"

When a mission statement already exists, you must review it and become expert in it. It is equally important to determine the extent to which the existing mission statement is in alignment with the executive sponsor's current goals and objectives for the organization.

The following assessment tool contains a series of questions you should be asking yourself and, when in doubt, verifying with the executive sponsor.

Assess an Existing Mission Statement

Things to Think About	Record Your Thoughts Here

Has the mission statement, as stated, been largely accomplished, or does it still represent a long-term target? What evidence exists?

Based on what you know of the executive sponsor's current goals and objectives, does it appear the existing mission statement will be acceptable with only some fine tuning, or should a mission statement rewrite be a major part of your strategic planning session? How would you justify your conclusions to the executive sponsor and to the strategic planning team?

Are there terms and wording in the mission statement that no longer fit because of organizational changes that have occurred since it was drafted?

Do employees and other stakeholders appear familiar with the existing mission statement? If "no" why not? If "yes" what do they like or dislike about it? What do they find unrealistic? What reasons do they give?

Assess Potential Members of Strategic Planning Team

As leader of the strategic planning effort, one of your personal critical success factors is to work with a team which comprises *stakeholders*—people (and groups) that have vested interests in the success of the organization.

The following assessment tool represents a two-step process to help you identify and assess potential planning team members.

Step One:

Look Within and Outside the Organization

The following assessment tool will help you and your executive sponsor think about potential stakeholder sources.

Have I Considered the Following Sources?

❑   Senior management

❑   Middle management

❑   Employee groups and organizations (e.g., unions)

❑   Customers

❑   Suppliers

❑   Distribution channels (e.g., distributors, marketing representatives)

❑   Existing (or potential) strategic partners and alliances

❑   Trade and professional organizations

Step Two:

Prioritize Potential Team Members You have Identified

Once you have identified potential team members, you need to assess the value of each, weeding out those with lessor potential since you won't be able to include everyone.

NOTE: *The points shown in the following table are somewhat arbitrary. You may wish to adjust them to reflect the realities and values of your organization.*

Team Member Evaluation Criteria Worksheet

Potential Team Member:_____

Evaluation Criteria	Points
Recommended or recognized by the executive sponsor as a valuable team member	10
Will be significantly impacted by the success or failure of the strategic planning changes	10
Has participated in other, successful strategic planning efforts	8
Wants to be a member of the strategic planning team	5
Is open-minded to new ideas	5
Has good interpersonal and communications skills	10
Is interested and willing to commit the required effort	10
Has existing, strong, fixed opinions about the future directions of the organization	−5
_____	_____
_____	_____
_____	_____
TOTAL:	_____

Process

Make one copy of "Team Member Evaluation Criteria Worksheet" on page 134 for each potential team member you have identified. Fill in the name. Then complete the worksheet. Space has been provided to add additional criteria you feel are important to your organization.

Those with the highest point totals are probably your best candidates for serving on the strategic planning team.

Set Two— *Session Assessments*

This set contains one participant assessment tool for each of the three sessions:

It also contains detailed instructions for administering each assessment.

00:10

One-hour Strategic Planning Meeting Assessment

Purposes

Allow participants the opportunity to evaluate the worth of this session, from their own and from their organization's perspective.

Collect suggestions and other feedback that will help you enhance future sessions.

FACILITATOR COMMENTARY

Individual assessment

 INTRODUCE the assessment.

> I am now going to ask you to complete a brief assessment of this session.
>
> The time you take will help me learn what worked well for you, and what I might do to make further sessions even more valuable and productive.
>
> Before you fill out the assessment, be sure to review the purpose of this strategic planning session, on top of the assessment worksheet.

 DISTRIBUTE the "One-hour Strategic Planning Meeting Assessment Worksheet" on page 138.

 REVIEW the instructions on the assessment with participants.

ALLOW 3-5 minutes for completion.

> **Procedural note:** *During the following discussion, ask participants to volunteer recommendations they feel most strongly about. Ask clarifying questions as needed.*

GROUP DISCUSSION

 ASK participants to volunteer their highest priority improvement recommendations.

 RECORD recommendations on a flipchart. When recommendations are complete:

CHECK OFF any which are addressed in the Half-day Strategic Planning Briefing, or in the One-day Strategic Planning Workshop.

 DESCRIBE the purpose and content of those session options as time permits.

THANK participants for their ideas and recommendations.

One-hour Strategic Planning Meeting Assessment Worksheet

The purpose of this session was: To explain the need for strategic planning, its objectives and worthwhile outcomes, and to review methodologies used during strategic planning.

Read the assessment questions and rate each by circling the appropriate number on the rating scale provided. Interpret the rating scale as follows:

7 *Exceeded* my and my organization's *expectations*

4 *Met* my and my organization's needs

1 *Inadequate* for my and my organization's *needs*.

Also, note specific, constructive recommendations you have for improving the session.

When you are finished, check off one to three recommendations you would give highest priority.

Assessment Question	Rating	Improvement Recommendations
I understand the elements of effective strategic planning.	1 2 3 4 5 6 7	
If asked, I could describe in my own terms the three phases of strategic planning and what each accomplishes.	1 2 3 4 5 6 7	
I can distinguish between project planning, tactical planning, and strategic planning.	1 2 3 4 5 6 7	
I can explain a process for evaluating the current status of my organization.	1 2 3 4 5 6 7	
I can identify and explain the terms "vision" and "mission statement" and can provide an example specific to my own organization.	1 2 3 4 5 6 7	
If asked, I could describe to others a general approach for establishing and achieving strategic planning objectives.	1 2 3 4 5 6 7	

00:15   ### *Half-day Strategic Planning Briefing Assessment*

Purposes   Allow participants the opportunity to evaluate this session's worth, from their own and their organization's perspective.

Collect suggestions and other feedback that will help you enhance future sessions.

Individual assessment   **FACILITATOR COMMENTARY**

INTRODUCE the assessment.

> I am now going to ask you to complete a brief assessment of this session.
>
> The time you take will help me learn what worked well for you, and what I might do to make further sessions even more valuable and productive.
>
> Before you fill out the assessment, be sure to review the purpose of this strategic planning session, as presented at the top of the assessment sheet.

DISTRIBUTE the "Half-day Strategic Planning Briefing Assessment Worksheet" on page 140.

REVIEW the instructions on the assessment with participants.

ALLOW 6-8 minutes for completion.

> **Procedural note:** *During the following discussion, ask participants to volunteer recommendations they feel most strongly about. Ask clarifying questions as needed.*

Group discussion

ASK participants to volunteer their highest priority improvement recommendations.

RECORD recommendations on a flipchart. When recommendations are complete:

CHECK OFF any which are addressed in the One-day Strategic Planning Workshop.

DESCRIBE the purpose and content of that session option as time permits.

THANK participants for their ideas and recommendations.

Half-day Strategic Planning Briefing Assessment Worksheet

The purpose of this session was: To introduce significant concepts associated with strategic planning, and to demonstrate techniques planners can use in their strategic planning.

Read the assessment questions and rate each by circling the appropriate number on the rating scale provided. Interpret the rating scale as follows:

7   *Exceeded* my and my organization's *expectations*

4   *Met* my and my organization's needs

1   *Inadequate* for my and my organization's needs.

Also, note specific, constructive recommendations you have for improving the session.

When you are finished, check off one to three recommendations you would give highest priority.

Assessment Question	Rating	Improvement Recommendations
I can list at least one significant change, arising from either within or outside of my organization, that is likely to necessitate change in the way we now operate.	1 2 3 4 5 6 7	_____
If asked, I could explain the typical growth cycle of any organization, and locate my own organization on that growth cycle curve.	1 2 3 4 5 6 7	_____
If asked, I could explain the idea of "growth cycle discontinuities" to one unfamiliar with the concept.	1 2 3 4 5 6 7	_____
I can explain some of the reasons leading to growth cycle discontinuities within an organization.	1 2 3 4 5 6 7	_____
I can distinguish between strategic and tactical planning, and explain how one relates to the other.	1 2 3 4 5 6 7	_____
I can explain how strategic planning can help an organization head off discontinuities in growth.	1 2 3 4 5 6 7	_____
I can define the term, Critical Success Factor, and provide an example from my own organization.	1 2 3 4 5 6 7	_____
I can distinguish between tactical planning and action planning.	1 2 3 4 5 6 7	_____

00:20   ***One-day Strategic Planning Workshop Assessment***

Purposes   Allow participants the opportunity to evaluate the worth of this session, from their own and from their organization's perspective.

Collect suggestions and other feedback that will help you enhance future sessions.

Individual assessment

 FACILITATOR COMMENTARY

INTRODUCE the assessment.

> I am now going to ask you to complete a brief assessment of this session.

> The time you take will help me learn what worked well for you, and what I might do to make further sessions even more valuable and productive.

> Before you fill out the assessment, be sure to review the instructions and purpose of this strategic planning session, as presented in the instructions at the top of the assessment sheet.

 DISTRIBUTE the "One-day Strategic Planning Workshop Assessment Worksheet" on page 142.

 REVIEW the instructions on the assessment with participants.

ALLOW 8-10 minutes for completion.

> **Procedural note:** *During the following discussion, ask participants to volunteer recommendations they feel most strongly about. Ask clarifying questions as needed*

Group discussion

 ASK participants to volunteer their highest priority improvement recommendations.

 RECORD recommendations on a flipchart. When recommendations are complete:

CHECK OFF any which are addressed in the half or one day strategic planning workshop.

DESCRIBE the purpose and content of those session options as time permits.

THANK participants for their ideas and recommendations.

One-day Strategic Planning Workshop
Assessment Worksheet

The purpose of this session was: To lead strategic planning teams through the major steps required to develop and begin implementing an effective strategic plan for their organization.

Read the assessment questions and rate each by circling the appropriate number on the rating scale provided. Interpret the rating scale as follows:

> 7   *Exceeded* my and my organization's *expectations*
>
> 4   *Met* my and my organization's needs
>
> 1   *Inadequate* for my and my organization's *needs*.

Also, note specific, constructive recommendations you have for improving the session.

When you are finished, check off one to three recommendations you would give highest priority.

Assessment Question	Rating	Improvement Recommendations
I believe my group has effectively described our organization's current status during this workshop.	1 2 3 4 5 6 7	_____
I can list at least five of my organization's key stakeholders, and explain why they are key to our strategic mission.	1 2 3 4 5 6 7	_____
If asked, I could list some of our organization's key strengths and weaknesses.	1 2 3 4 5 6 7	_____
If asked, I could suggest some opportunities for my organization's continuing success.	1 2 3 4 5 6 7	_____
If asked, I could identify some potential threats to my organization's continuing success.	1 2 3 4 5 6 7	_____
The visioning procedure used during this workshop helped clarify my organization's strategic direction, or identified potential alternatives to our current direction.	1 2 3 4 5 6 7	_____
The mission statements developed during this workshop helped clarify my organization's strategic direction.	1 2 3 4 5 6 7	_____
As a result of this workshop, our group has clear, specific action plans to begin working toward the achievement of our strategic plan.	1 2 3 4 5 6 7	_____
If asked, I could describe several of the factors critical to the success (CSFs) of our strategic plan, as well as several of the critical assumptions upon which those CSFs are based.	1 2 3 4 5 6 7	_____

Set Three— *Results, Progress Assessments*

This set contains assessment tools to help you monitor progress and redirect efforts toward achievement of the strategic plan.

Assess Action Plan Progress

The assessment questions participants answered at the end of each strategic planning session were intended to measure their satisfaction with the session. Even more important to the success of strategic planning is to monitor and measure the results of the team's strategic planning efforts *subsequent to* the planning sessions:

> Are the action plan activities occurring? On time?
>
> Are the desired outcomes of the action plan being realized?
>
> What mid-course corrective changes are needed, if any?
>
> What real progress is being made toward the new mission?

If you are the strategic planning executive sponsor, you should be asking yourself these questions. If you are a consultant to the organization, you should be asking the executive sponsor these questions—and supporting his or her efforts to make the strategic plans a reality.

Timing is important. The strategic planning team should have enough time to accomplish initial efforts. However, not too much time should elapse before a review takes place, or the momentum of the effort will be lost. Typically, organizations conduct progress reviews after 30 days and again after 90 days.

> **NOTE:** *While we have used those time intervals for the worksheets that follow, feel free to select whatever intervals make sense in your own organization.*

The following materials contain sample worksheets to accomplish a 30-day and a 90-day assessment, together with instructions for using the worksheets.

30-day Action Plan Assessment Worksheet

Use this worksheet to structure your assessment of action plan progress after about 30 days. For any question to which the answer is *no*, you should meet with the appropriate individual(s). It may be the entire group, or it may be the person assigned to carry out a specific activity.

30-day Action Planning Review Worksheet

Assessment Question	Result	Comments, Recommendations
If action plans were not completed during the strategic planning training session, are they now complete and available for review?	❑ Yes ❑ No	
Has the action plan been reviewed and approved by the executive sponsor?	❑ Yes ❑ No	
Have new action plan activities been added?	❑ Yes ❑ No	
If new action plan activities have been added, does the action plan still appear to be in alignment with the agreed-upon mission statement?	❑ Yes ❑ No	
Is a specific individual identified with the responsibility of ensuring that each action plan activity takes place?	❑ Yes ❑ No	
Have other human and monetary resources been allocated?	❑ Yes ❑ No	
Do people assigned to the project understand their roles and responsibilities?	❑ Yes ❑ No	
Are the outcomes associated with each activity expected business results (not just a restatement of the activity)?	❑ Yes ❑ No	
Is a target completion date assigned for each activity? Is it realistic?	❑ Yes ❑ No	

90-day Action Plan Assessment Worksheet

Use this two-step worksheet to structure your assessment of action plan progress after about 90 days. In this assessment you should be concerned with progress and results. Is the organization's new mission (as defined during the strategic planning session) being realized? What, if anything, is impeding progress? What can be done about it?

If you are the executive sponsor, use this worksheet to debrief your team members and to fine-tune strategic planning efforts.

If you are a consultant supporting the executive sponsor, review this worksheet with the sponsor, and help him/her plan a course of attack to achieve the mission statement.

90-day Action Planning Review Worksheet—Step One

Assessment Question	Activity Item #	Activity Description	Apparent Reasons
Which activity items that should have been completed are not?			
Which activity items are seriously behind schedule?			
Are there activities and milestones that will be critical to the mission's success? If so list them.			

In preparation for step two, list each incomplete or behind-schedule activity and activity number from the *step one worksheet* onto a *separate step two worksheet*. (Make as many copies as needed.) Then complete each *step two worksheet*.

Looking ahead

The actions you list in the Action column of the "90-day Action Planning Review Worksheet—Step Two" form the basis for the next 90 day action plan.

90-day Action Planning Review Worksheet—Step Two

Item Number: _____   Activity: _____

Assessment Item	Action
❑ This activity item is behind schedule because it is dependent upon completion of another activity item.	If checked, concentrate your efforts on the prior activity items. If not, continue to the next question.
❑ This activity is behind schedule for lack of resources.	If checked, list possible resources that can be made available. If not, note what else can be done to accelerate completion. For instance, you should determine whether all people assigned are still performing.
❑ This activity item is behind schedule due to outside influences.	If checked, identify the outside cause and list the action(s) you will take to overcome the problem. If not, identify the other cause(s) and list actions you will take to overcome the problem.
❑ I'll need to enlist the executive sponsor's support to get the process back on track.	If checked, schedule a meeting to present your new action plan. If not, implement your action plan to move ahead.

Chapter Eight:

Overhead Transparencies

This Chapter

…contains master overhead transparencies for sessions the book describes. Photocopy them onto overhead transparency material, enlarging or reducing them to fit your projector.

Use these as published, or modify them to meet your specific requirements.

The master overhead transparencies which follow are arranged in the following order:

One-
hour
Strategic
Planning
Visuals

What Are the Meeting Objectives?

- Overview the strategic planning process

- Introduce key terms used throughout the strategic planning process

- Overview key steps involved in strategic planning

- Discuss the need for, and major benefits of, strategic planning

151

Types of Plans

- **Project Plans**
  Describe the detailed activities, responsibilities, and targeted completion dates required to complete a specific project

- **Tactical Plans**
  Describe overall activities, measurable outcomes, responsibilities, and targeted completion dates required to succeed during a relatively short period of time (such as a one-year period)

- **Strategic Plans**
  Describe the overall directions and targeted outcomes required to achieve the organization's mission. Require the organization to take a longer term (three to five year) perspective

- **Action Plans**
  Short-range plans developed to identify activities, outcomes, responsible individuals, and target dates required to measure the organization's success in achieving its mission, goals, and objectives

152

How Do Action Plans Relate to the Mission, & to Other Plans?

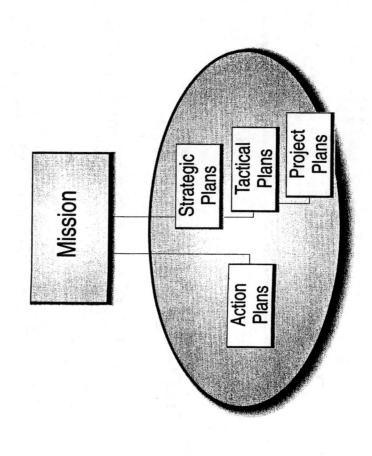

How Will We Develop Our Organizational Strategic Plan?

Strategic Planning Approach

Phase I: Determine where we are as an organization

Phase II: Decide where we would like to be

Phase III: Establish an approach to achieve our target, and implement it

How Will We Evaluate Where We Are Now?

Stakeholders   Individuals and/or groups that are significantly impacted by success or failure of the organization

Strengths   Areas of value within our organization and stakeholder groups

Weaknesses   Liabilities within our organization and stakeholder groups

Opportunities   Favorable or advantageous combinations of circumstances that provide the organization opportunities to explore new directions

Threats   Possible risks that could threaten the viability and future success of our organization

How Will We Determine Where We Want to Be?

- ## Vision

  A mental picture of what the organization should look like in the future, and how the organization will look, feel, and interact with its stakeholders

- ## Mission

  A formal statement describing the future direction of the organization, consistent with the values, goals, and objectives of the stakeholder groups.

156

How Will We Establish an Approach to Achieve, Implement Target?

Critical Assumptions
Key assumptions upon which the organization bases future direction

Critical Success Factors
The few, high-priority areas which the organization must manage to be successful

Outcomes
Observable results that provide evidence that critical success factors are being achieved

Activities
Actions that result in or contribute to an outcome

What Is Our Action Plan?

What	Intensive strategic planning session
Why	Establish a longer-term view of organizational direction, and define plans to implement it
When	_____ (date, time)
Where	_____ (location)
Who	_____ [stakeholder name(s)]
How	Strategic planning approach
Facilitators	_____ (facilitator names)
References	_____ (relevant organizational documents, such as existing mission statement, organizational charts, etc.)

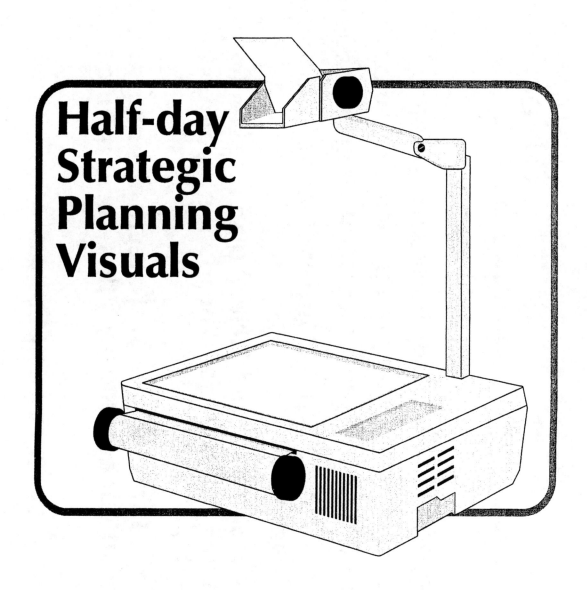

Half-day Strategic Planning Visuals

Objectives

- Define key terms related to strategic planning

- Recognize significant changes impacting organizations

- Recognize the typical growth cycle of an organization

- Recognize discontinuities in a growth cycle, and explain possible causes

- Explain how strategic and tactical planning can help organizations anticipate and head off operational discontinuities

- Describe the three phases of strategic planning and the typical activities and processes that occur during each phase

Change

" ... do it better, make it better, improve it even if it ain't broke, because if we don't we can't compete with those who do. "

Masaaki Imai, KAIZEN

Accelerating Demands

- **Customer requirements and satisfaction**
- **Increased competition**
- **Cycle time reduction**
- **Cost reduction**
- **Down-sizing and right-sizing**
- **Environmental considerations**
- **Social and cultural issues**
- **Globalization**

Growth Curve

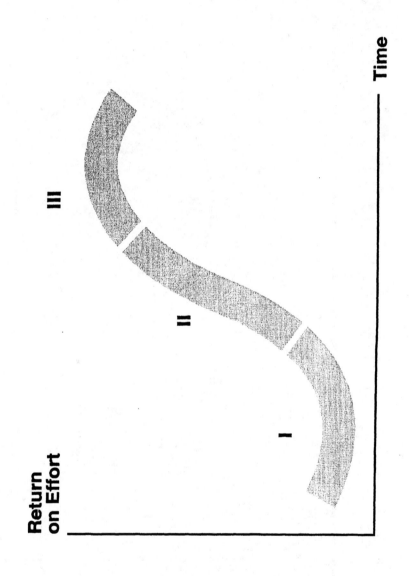

Return on Effort

Time

Growth Curve Discontinuity

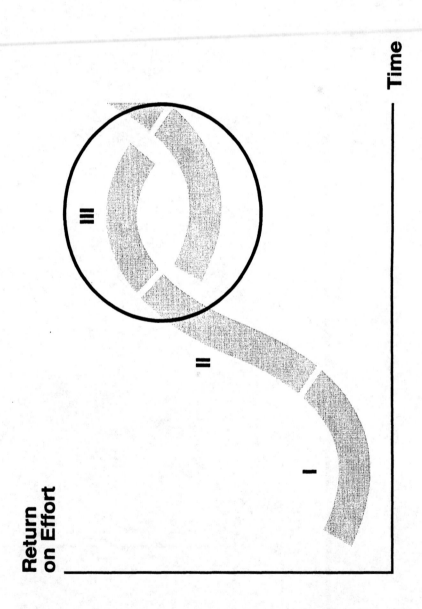

Return on Effort

Time

Some Working Definitions

- Strategic Planning
- Tactical Planning
- Project Planning
- Action Planning

The Strategic Planning Journey (1)

Phase I   **Determine where you are now**

Phase II   **Decide where you want to be**

Phase III   **Establish a strategy to achieve your target**

Where Are You Now?

- Identify stakeholders

- Identify *strengths, weaknesses, opportunities, and threats* (SWOT)

- Identify core values

Stakeholder Analysis

Stakeholder (definition)

Individual or other organization that will be positively or negatively affected by the success or failure of an organization

Examples

Employees

Customers/clients

Suppliers

SWOT Analysis

- **Strengths (SWOT)**

- **Weaknesses (SWOT)**

- **Opportunities (SWOT)**

- **Threats (SWOT)**

Value Analysis

Values (definition)

- An organization's basic beliefs
- Underlying principles which are the basis for all (or at least most) of the organization's vision, strategies, plans, policies, and actions

Examples

- Respect for the *individual*
- Best customer service
- Excellence in execution

The Strategic Planning Journey (2)

Phase I   Determine where you are now

Phase II Decide where you want to be

Phase III Establish a strategy to achieve your target

Where Do You Want to Be?

- Create a *vision*

- Establish a *mission statement*

The Vision

Vision (definition)

- A mental picture of what the organization should look like, feel like, and be seen as in the future
- A valuable set of ideas that allows stakeholders to negotiate individual ideas into a *shared vision*

Examples:

- Organization is featured in Business Week for its exemplary approach to meeting current organizational requirements through extraordinary measures
- Organization is recognized by the country's chief executive for its contribution to improving nation's public education

173

Sample Mission Statements

- *Blue Cross/Blue Shield* of Maryland is a comprehensive managed health-care insurance company that manages the quality of health care, service, and the costs of its offerings to individuals and groups. To serve customers effectively, BC/BS offers a portfolio of products and administrative services, with emphasis on managed care.

- *Texas Instruments'* Enterprise Solutions Division specializes in re-engineered application solutions for enterprise materials management, electronic commerce, and advanced manufacturing.

The Strategic Planning Journey (3)

Phase I   Determine where you are now

Phase II   Decide where you want to be

Phase III   Establish a strategy to achieve your target

What Strategy Will You Use?

- Identify strategic approach

- Identify strategic opportunities

- Prioritize opportunities

Porter Generic Strategy Model

	Cost Leadership	Differentiation
Total Market Focus		
Niche Market Focus		

Strategic Alignment

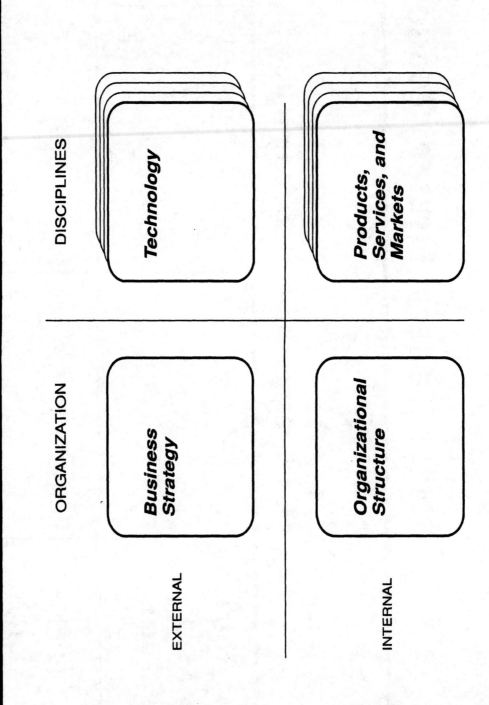

DISCIPLINES

ORGANIZATION

Technology

Products, Services, and Markets

Business Strategy

Organizational Structure

EXTERNAL

INTERNAL

178

Reaching the Vision

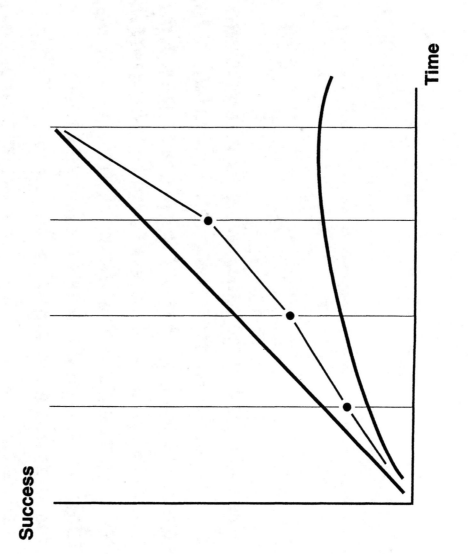

Change

" *It can be very hard in any organization to change mind sets. It may be even harder to stop people extrapolating from the status quo. Ironically, it is often the very best firms that are most locked into old views and established ideas. Their sense of cohesion leads them, if not to smugness, then to a tendency to resist any challenge to the assumptions that have brought them success. Their industry leadership makes it hard for them to imagine that anyone outside the industry can be a threat. Past achievements make them overconfident in forecasting.* "

Peter G. W. Keen, Competing in Time

How Will You Implement Your Plans?

- **Identify Critical Assumptions**

- **Identify Critical Success Factors (CSFs)**

- **Create Action Plans**

The Strategic Planning Journey (4)

Phase I   Determine where you are now

Phase II   Decide where you want to be

Phase III   Establish a strategy to achieve your target

Implement your strategy by creating and enacting required tactical plans

Critical Assumptions

Critical Assumptions (definition)

The few, key assumptions on which the organization is basing its plans

Examples:

The organization's mission will remain unchanged for at least two years

The organization's operating budget will be reduced by 20 percent per year for the next three years

The economy will grow an annual 10 percent and inflation will not exceed 3 percent

Identifying Critical Assumptions

- **Group One Situation**

  Part of your strategic plan will entail the application of an emerging technology. Your organization does not own the patents, but you have a history of success working with the organization that does.

- **Group Two Situation**

  To achieve your strategic plan, over the next five years you plan to hire 120 recent Ph.D. graduates in genetic engineering.

184

Critical Success Factors (CSFs)

Definition:

- Those few key areas where things must go just right for the organization to flourish

- Characteristics, conditions, and variables that, when properly maintained and managed, can most positively impact an organization's success

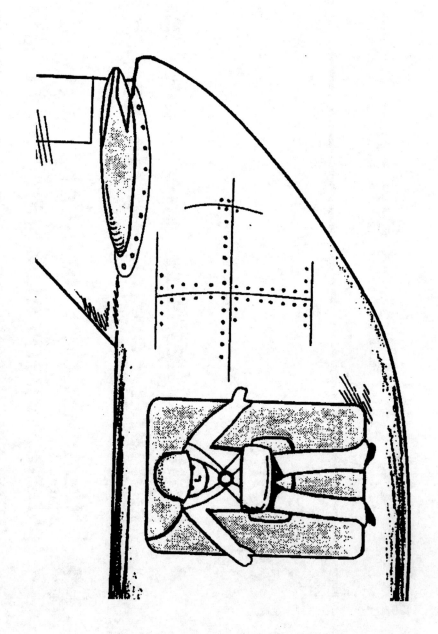

CSFs— During the Jump

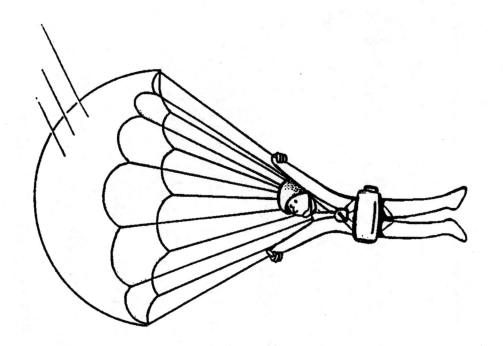

Example CSFs

Not-for-profit organization

- Funding
- Public relations
- Compliance with laws
- Trained staff
- Accountability
- Productivity
- Service orientation

Action Planning

An Action Plan:

- *Organizes and identifies support for and commitment to the mission*
- Used to energize participants on the actions needed to execute the plan AND gain their commitment to take responsibility for appropriate parts of the plan
- Provides time frames for observing and tracking activities and outcomes required to achieve an objective

An Action Plan is

- Not a task list
- Not a to-do list

Action Planning Approach

- **Describe project**

- **Define the desired project goal and objective(s)**

- **Set (or estimate) the end date**

- **Establish date when each outcome will be completed**

- **Identify who will be responsible for each outcome**

- **Establish completion date for each outcome**

- **Specify actions required to complete each outcome**

- **Determine immediate actions (to get the process started)**

The Action Plan

ACTION PLAN

Creation Date: _____

- 5 DAY
- 90 DAY

Description of Project _____

Project End Date: _____

Item	Outcome	By Whom	By When	Activity

One-day
Strategic
Planning
Visuals

One-day Strategic Planning Workshop

Purpose: *To lead this strategic planning team through the major steps required to develop and begin implementing an effective strategic plan*

Date and Time _____

Facilitator(s) _____

Long-term Success Is Within Reach, but Not in Our Grasp

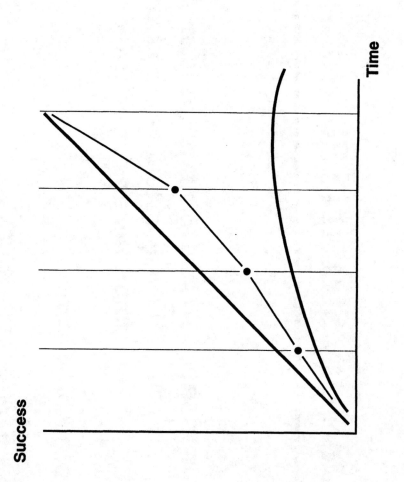

Success

Time

Create Organization's Strategic Plan

Strategic plans Describe overall directions and targeted outcomes required to achieve the organization's mission. They require the organization to take a longer term (three to five year) perspective

Tactical plans Describe overall activities, measurable outcomes, responsibilities, and targeted completion dates required to succeed during a relatively short period (such as one year)

Project Plans Describe detailed activities, responsibilities, deliverables, and targeted completion dates required to complete a specified project

Action plans Describe short-range courses of action the planning team commits to in implementing the strategic plan

Identify Our Stakeholders, Strengths, Weaknesses, Opportunities, & Threats

Stakeholders Individuals and/or groups that the success or failure of the organization will significantly affect

Strengths Assets (valuable resources) that exist within our organization and among our stakeholders

Weaknesses Liabilities that exist within our organization and among our stakeholders

Opportunities Favorable or advantageous combinations of circumstances that provide the organization with the chance to explore new directions

Threats Possible dangers that could threaten the viability and future success of our organization

SWOT Analysis: Look Internally, Externally

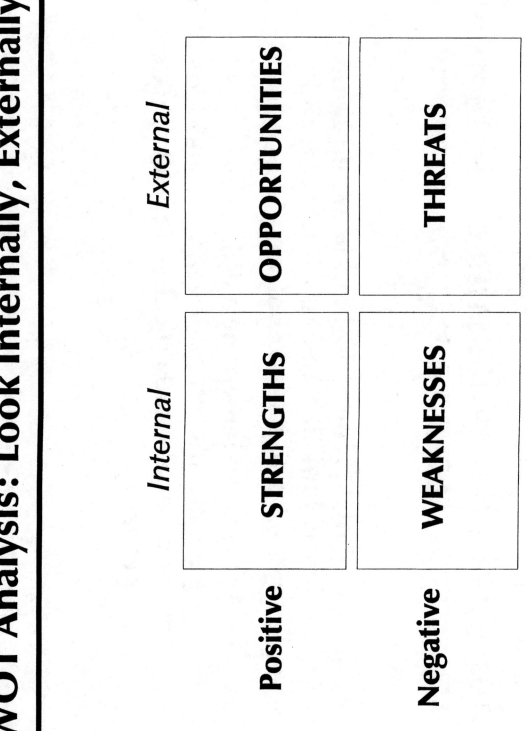

	Internal	External
Positive	STRENGTHS	OPPORTUNITIES
Negative	WEAKNESSES	THREATS

Create a Vision, Write Mission Statement

Vision

A mental picture of what the organization should look like and how it will feel and interact with its stakeholders

Mission statement

A formal statement describing the organization's future direction, consistent with values, goals, and objectives of stakeholders as a group

To Create a Vision, Change Your Frame of Reference

FROM

Today   ➜   The future

Looking forward ➜ Looking backward

Current circumstances ➜ Future success

Current assumptions
that yielded past
success ➜ Assumptions required
to achieve future
success

TO

Visioning Exercises
Create a View of Future Success

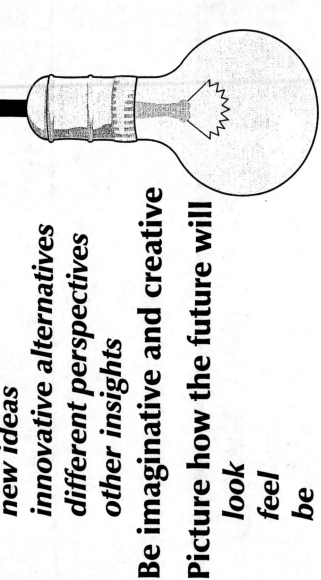

Create

new ideas

innovative alternatives

different perspectives

other insights

Be imaginative and creative

Picture how the future will

look

feel

be

To Be Creative, We Must Act Roles

Artist

Warrior

Explorer

Judge

Adapted from Roger von Oech, *A Kick in the Seat of the Pants*, New York, N.Y., Harper & Row, 1986

To Be Creative, We Must Act Roles (2)

Adapted from Roger von Oech, *A Kick in The Seat of The Pants*, New York, N.Y., Harper & Row, 1986

Explorer

Artist

Warrior

Judge

Before Creating Our Vision, We Must Be in a Creative Mood

B S A I N X L E A T N T E A R S

Visioning Exercises Involve Thinking About the Future and Picturing Results

- I will read you a few questions

- Relax and make yourself comfortable

- Close your eyes and breathe slowly

- Think freely about the questions

A Mission Statement Describes the Organization's Long-term Direction

- Is an organization's battle cry or rallying point

- Helps define how the organization will achieve its vision

No One Correct Mission Statement Style

"To provide memories"   **Fuji Film**

"Better things for better living through chemistry"   **DuPont**

"Beauty"   **Shiseido Cosmetics**

"ISPI is a preferred source of information education, and advocacy to enhance the tangible and enduring impact it is having on people, organizations, and the profession"   **ISPI***

*ISPI: International Society for Performance Improvement

Mission Statement Includes *Vision, Measurement, Theme*

—Peter Drucker & Russell Ackoff

Vision—Describes what the organization needs to accomplish, what products and services it will provide (or intends to), and what significant contribution it expects to make.

Measurement—Identifies ways in which progress can be measured.

Theme—Describes how the organization intends to achieve its goals. This helps distinguish your organization from others by defining its unique characteristics.

Questions Help Us Form Mission Statement

What should we be doing? . . . . **Vision**

What should the results be? . . . . **Vision**

What standards should we use? . . . . **Measurement**

How should this benefit stakeholders? . . . . **Theme**

Identify Opportunities, CSFs, Critical Assumptions

—Then Develop Action Plans

Opportunities—Favorable or advantageous combinations of circumstances that provide the chance to explore new directions

Critical Success Factors—The few, priority areas that an organization must manage to be successful

Critical Assumptions—The key assumptions upon which the organization is basing its plans

Action plans—Short-range actions identify activities, outcomes, responsible individuals, and target dates needed to implement business plans. Action plans communicate the status and progress of business plans.

Identify CSFs for Vision, Mission Statements

Now You Need an Action Plan

- **Provides time frames for observing and tracking activities and outcomes**

- **Organizes and identifies support for, and commitment to, these activities**

- **Not a task list, not a to-do list**

1997—2002						
5	6	7	1	2	3	4
12	13	14	8	9	10	11
19	20	21	15	16	17	18
26	27	28	22	23	24	25
			29	30	31	

Create Action Plan, Gain Commitment

- **Describe project**

- **Define project goal and objective(s)**

- **Set (or estimate) an end date**

- **Establish desired outcomes (milestones)**

- **Identify who will be responsible for each outcome**

- **Establish completion date for each outcome**

- **Specify activities required for each outcome**

- **Determine actions needed to get process started**

The Action Plan

Creation Date: _____

- 5 DAY
- 90 DAY

ACTION PLAN

Description of Project _____

Project End Date: _____

Item	Outcome	By Whom	By When	Activity

Now We Must Commit to Meeting the Vision, Mission

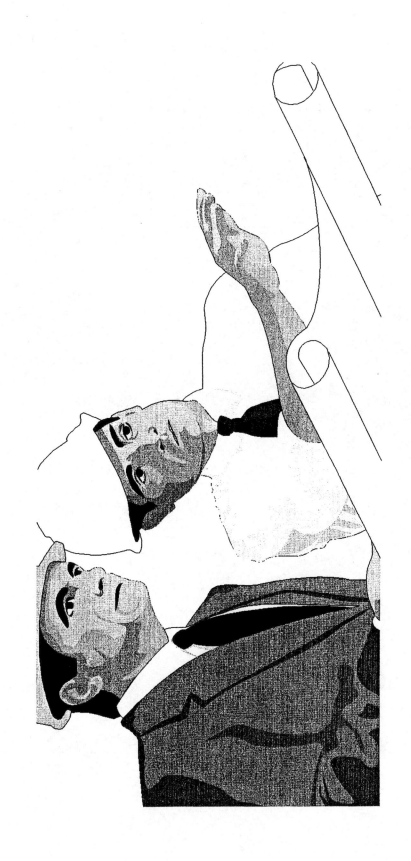

Chapter Nine:

Prepared Flipcharts

Prepare your flipcharts in advance:

> You will have one less task to perform during your strategic planning session.

> The headings will provide you transitional and introductory comment cues.

> Prepared flipcharts reflect good organizational structure to team members.

This Chapter

...contains masters of each of the prepared flipcharts we recommend. You can turn these masters into prepared flipcharts by:

> Copying the text by hand onto flipcharts, or

> Using the pages as masters in a flipchart/poster-making device.

Here are some suggestions for preparing the flipcharts:

> Be certain the flipcharts are legible.

> *Leave a blank page between each prepared flipchart.* In that way, the copy on the next flipchart in the pad will not be visible through the one you are currently using. In addition, the blank pages sometimes come in handy to record spontaneous ideas and comments.

The flipchart masters which follow are arranged in the following order:

CSFs/Outcomes

Critical Success Factors	Outcomes

AGENDA

❒ **Introduction**

❒ **Meeting a Changing World**

❒ **Organizational Growth Cycle**

❒ **Some Planning Concepts**

❒ **Strategic Planning Methodology**

❒ **Wrap-up**

Deterrents to Growth

From Within

_____

_____

_____

_____

_____

_____

From Outside

_____

_____

_____

_____

_____

_____

OUR KEY STAKEHOLDERS

OUR STRENGTHS & WEAKNESSES

Strengths	Weaknesses

EXAMPLES OF ORGANIZATIONAL STRENGTHS, WEAKNESSES

Strengths	Weaknesses

OUR OPPORTUNITIES AND THREATS

Opportunities	Threats

OUR STRENGTHS AND WEAKNESSES

Strengths	Weaknesses

EXAMPLES OF OPPORTUNITIES AND THREATS

Opportunities	Threats

OUR CORE VALUES

AGENDA

☐ **Introduction**

☐ **Phase I:**
> *Determine Where We Are Now*

☐ **Phase II:**
> *Decide Where We Would like to Be*

☐ **Phase III:**
> *Establish and Implement an Approach to Achieving Our Target*

☐ **Wrap-up**

THREE-PHASED APPROACH

□ **Phase I** **Determine where we are as an organization**

□ **Phase II** **Decide where we would like the organization to be**

□ **Phase III** **Establish and implement the approach to achieving our target**

OUR STAKEHOLDERS (FOR-PROFIT)

Customers

Stockholders

OUR STAKEHOLDERS (NONPROFIT)

Members

Board of Directors

OUR ORGANIZATION'S STRENGTHS

OUR ORGANIZATION'S WEAKNESSES

_____

_____

_____

_____

_____

_____

_____

_____

_____

_____

OUR ORGANIZATION'S OPPORTUNITIES

OUR ORGANIZATION'S THREATS

MISSION STATEMENT (FOR-PROFIT)

---

*"*Be the company that everyone wants to work for; everyone wants to do business with; everyone wants to own*"*

**Australian
Iron Ore
Producer**

Mission Statement (Nonprofit)

"...a humanitarian organization, led by volunteers, that provides relief to victims of disasters and helps people prevent, prepare for, and respond to emergencies"

American Red Cross

OUR BEST OPPORTUNITIES

OUR MISSION STATEMENT

OUR CRITICAL SUCCESS FACTORS

OUR CRITICAL ASSUMPTIONS

ACTION PLAN

☐   **5 day**
☐   **90 day**

Creation Date _____

Project Description

_____

_____

_____

Project End Date _____

Item	Outcome	By Whom?	By When?	Activity

Glossary

Acronyms

CSF—Critical Success Factor

SWOT—see *SWOT analysis*

Words

action plans—short range courses of action developed to identify *activities, outcomes, responsible individuals,* and *target dates* needed to implement any kind of business plan. Action plans are useful tools for communicating to management the *status* and *progress* of any business plan.

activities—actions that result in, or contribute to, an *outcome.*

critical assumptions—the few, key presumptions on which the organization is basing its plans.

critical success factors—the few, high-priority areas which the organization must manage well to be successful. Note the words *critical* and *few.*

executive sponsor—key management person within the organization that wants to have the strategic planning session conducted. This individual must have a *healthy dissatisfaction* with the organization's current situation and must be ready to lead the effort to achieve the vision developed during or as a result of the session(s).

facilitator—leads people in new directions, drawing out independent ideas, and achieving a *level of consensus.* Facilitator accepts the critical role of helping an organization make some of the most important decisions it can make. Facilitator's role is not passive, is hard work.

healthy dissatisfaction—the key executive and/or executive sponsor is unhappy with the status quo and believes change is necessary if the organization is to succeed and grow. (Compare with *unhealthy attitude.*)

mission statement—describes the *future direction* of the organization. It should be consistent with the *values, goals,* and *objectives* of the organization's stakeholders.

opportunity—favorable or advantageous *combinations* of *circumstances* that provide the chance to explore new directions.

247

outcomes—the observable results of activities.

project plan—the most commonly developed plans and, therefore, the type of planning with which most of us have the more experience. Project plans have very tangible and measurable outcomes. The duration is generally fixed, with a specified *starting date* and a targeted *completion date*.

stakeholders—individuals and functions that are or will be affected by the organization's successes and failures. May include individuals from other organizations.

strategic plan—defines the actions required to successfully achieve the organization's targeted outcomes over a time frame, typically three to five years.

strategic planning sessions—elicit from participants a plan which will lead the organization in an effective new strategic direction. Strategic planning is appropriate for both for-profit and nonprofit-oriented organizations.

SWOT analysis—(pronounced *swat*) defines organization's *strengths, weaknesses, opportunities,* and *threats* to success. Answers the question "Where are we now?"

tactical plan—supports strategic plans. Tactical plans are measurable, assign *responsibilities*, and specify *completion dates*. Typical tactical plans have believable, relatively short time frames such as *six to eighteen months*.

threats—situations that could threaten an organization's viability or future success.

unhealthy attitude—the sense, from a key executive who might serve as an executive sponsor, that all hope of future success is gone; or from someone who is *sufficiently satisfied* with the current situation to be unwilling to exert the effort to achieve change.

values—an organization's basic beliefs or underlying principles which are the basis for all (or most) of the organization's *vision, strategies, plans, policies,* and *actions*.

vision—a mental picture of what an organization should look like in the future. It may include a view of how the organization will look and feel, and how it will interact with *stakeholders*.

visioning—process that entails establishing a vision for the organization. This vision is then documented in the form of a formal, written, mission statement endorsed by all on the planning team. Neither *vision* nor *mission statements* indicate how to get there. Those statements identify where the organization wants to go and what they want to be in the future.

Index

About the Author

John Wills is president and CEO of Los Angeles based FLI, Incorporated. John provides consulting in the areas of strategic and tactical planning, sales, sales management, marketing, information systems, consulting methodology, training, and documentation. FLI is an award-winning performance technology consulting firm and represents over 150 independent consultants who are members of the FLI Professional Affiliates Network (FLI-*net*™). John co-founded FLI in 1980 and has provided the business acumen it needed to flourish, including the strategic and tactical planning guidance.

John is a recognized leader in using innovative approaches to help organizations develop strategic and tactical plans. John, together with FLI and its affiliates, has helped hundreds of large and small organizations implement practical, organization-specific plans in Asia, Australia, Europe, and North and South America. In addition, John is an active participant with a number of professional organizations and is currently the Strategic Planning Committee chairperson, International Society for Performance Improvement (ISPI).

Acknowledgments

I would like to thank Van O. Wright for his ideas and invaluable contribution to the preparation of this book. I would also like to acknowledge the assistance of Herbert R. Miller, Steven Berry, and Anne Coyle for their encouragement and suggestions. Equally, I would like to thank the many clients who helped us develop this strategic planning approach by adding ideas and by applying them to their organizations.

"KNOWLEDGE AND HUMAN POWER ARE SYNONYMOUS"

Knowledge generates human performance. It doesn't take a famous quote or the picture of a tree to know that. But full potential requires the proper elements. Your professional growth can thrive, as a member of the American Society for Training and Development.

As an ASTD member you will get:

Information on the forefront of practice and technology

Access to colleagues around the world for idea-sharing

Opportunity to contribute to the advancement of your profession

through...international conferences and expositions...best practices...electronic resources and networking...benchmarking publications...personalized research assistance...and much more.

Join ASTD now...and become part of a worldwide association of nearly 58,000 leaders in the field of workplace learning and performance.

Call 703.683.8100. Or fax 703.683.1523
Mention Priority Code: MH5A
TDD: 703.683.4323

 ASTD
AMERICAN SOCIETY
FOR TRAINING AND
DEVELOPMENT

Delivering Performance in a Changing World